Writing Naturally

Writing Naturally

A Memoir

William Sargent

UNIVERSITY PRESS OF NEW ENGLAND
HANOVER AND LONDON

Published by University Press of New England,
One Court Street, Lebanon, NH 03766
www.upne.com
© 2006 by University Press of New England
Printed in the United States of America

5 4 3 2 1

Library of Congress Cataloging-in-Publication Data
Sargent, William, 1946–
Writing naturally : a memoir / William Sargent.
p. cm.
ISBN-13: 978-1-58465-468-1 (cloth : alk. paper)
ISBN-10: 1-58465-468-6 (cloth : alk. paper)
1. Sargent, William, 1946– 2. Naturalists—United States—Biography.
3. Natural history literature—United States. 4. Natural
history—Authorship. I. Title.
QH31.S185
[A3 2006]
508.092—dc22 2006008643

 University Press of New England is a member of the Green Press Initiative. The paper used in this book meets their minimum requirements for recycled paper.

Contents

Preface

In 2004, I received a call from a former classmate at Harvard University. Would I be able to fill in for Al Gore, who had been called away at the last minute to attend Ronald Reagan's funeral? Our class needed someone to talk about global warming for our thirty-fifth reunion. Besides the unexpected honor, the event brought back a flood of memories.

In 1965, I had sat beside Al Gore in "Gov 1a," Harvard's introductory government course. We quickly learned that we had a lot in common. We had both been strongly influenced by growing up in rural areas, we had both gone to school in Washington, D.C., and we were both interested in environmental matters. But we had something else in common as well. In fact, all the freshmen in that class soon learned we had something else in common. Almost all of our parents were either in office or in government service. Al Gore's father was the senior senator from Tennessee, and my father was the lieutenant governor of Massachusetts.

Now, I don't think I'm disclosing any deep, dark, state secret when I reveal that certain members of Harvard's government department have been known to select students based solely on the basis of who they thought would someday hold influential government jobs. If that is so, I fear Al Gore was a great success and I was a dismal failure.

While Al Gore dutifully stayed in the government department, I fell happily into biological anthropology, where section leaders were known more for filling their classes with attractive Radcliffe students rather than with political wannabes. While Al studied government, I took a year off to study plankton on a six-month cruise to Africa, South America, and the Baltic. While Lieutenant Gore served in Vietnam, I studied monkeys on an island off Puerto Rico. While Congressman Gore ran for Senate, I set up a marine lab on Cape Cod. While Senator Gore ran for President, I helped produce films and wrote books about horseshoe crabs, bioterrorism, and sea-level rise.

Of course, I opened my talk by thanking my classmates for inviting me to speak, but pointed out, "Of course, I shouldn't really be here.

In fact, none of us should really be at Harvard today. We should all be having our reunion in the White House waiting for President Gore to take a few minutes out of his busy schedule to talk to speak to us about global warming." Did I know my audience or what?

But my talk made me realize that there actually had been a pattern to my seemingly haphazard life. When in doubt, I had entered some establishment endeavor like going to law school, before realizing that I had to just let my writing guide me naturally through life.

The process has not always been easy, but gradually I have found that following my writing has led me through a fascinating and enjoyable life. I have even recently discovered that during all those years when I thought I was just lurching from project to project, I was actually helping to create a coherent, even sexy new field called science writing, which is now being taught in schools of journalism!

Science writing has allowed me to observe and sometimes participate in biology as it has emerged from being a musty little academic backwater populated by avuncular practitioners in tweedy attire, to potentially the most powerful scientific field to ever shape human society. Every day, scientists grapple with technologies whose godlike capabilities stand to reshape life and the earth as we know it. Every day, biologists must deal with issues that will determine whether our species, or even our planet, has a future. As a science writer, I have been able to travel the world and meet people immersed in these questions—people still fascinated with the miracles of existence and our universe.

The more I talk to colleagues, the more I realize that there is no secret path that will lead inexorably and inevitably toward science writing. Some have come to the field from doing research in the hard sciences, others from English literature, some from covering the state house. Some even come from journalism schools.

But perhaps that is the point, after all. Most people don't get into science writing by plotting out an artificial, well-defined path; they get here by simply letting their writing lead them naturally where it will. If that is so, then here is my life, a life guided by writing naturally.

Writing Naturally

Chapter 1

Beginnings

Pleasant Bay (1950s)

My early childhood was semi-idyllic—idyllic in summer, and semi in winter. I was born in 1946 on Cape Cod, where my father had settled after he fought with the U.S. ski troops during World War II. My parents, Francis and Jessie, were regarded as the hippies of their generation. My father built their house, while running a fishing boat, starting a sporting goods store, and generally rebelling against his own straight-laced New England upbringing. Shortly after I was born, my father took the governor of Massachusetts, Robert Bradford, on a fishing trip. Pup talked the governor's ear off about how bad the conservation laws were and how nobody paid any attention to them anyway. These were themes he had also been writing about in the local Cape Cod newspapers.

A few weeks later, the governor called to ask if my father would like to be Commissioner of Marine Fisheries for the state of Massachusetts. Pup said he would, but only on the condition that he could return to fishing when the season started up again in the spring. He held the job without interruption for the next 15 years. From my point of view, the unfortunate result of this change in my father's work status was that we went from living year-round on Cape-Cod to spending the winters in Dover, a leafy suburb outside of Boston. But we returned every summer, all summer long, to my beloved Cape Cod.

During those early summers I came truly alive. Each day would start with the first rays of sunlight streaming into my upstairs bedroom. I would slip into my skimpiest bathing suit and tiptoe downstairs, to avoid waking my slumbering family. But it was a battle I generally lost. In my eagerness to rush outside I would burst through the screen door, which would inevitably slam shut behind me, provoking at least one member of the family to bellow, "Billy, go back to bed! Can't anybody do something about that damn child?"

My first mission was to pick the tomatoes that grew in a row beneath my sister's bedroom window. They thrived there, bathed in the first shimmering light of day, yet protected by the lee of the house. The vines were beaded with sunlit dew, each droplet caught in the tiny hairs of a succulent leaf. As I brushed through the vines, I was enveloped in the odor of their leaves. It was the tangy smell of the earth, the sun, of summer itself.

I plucked a tomato and bit into its red, sun-warmed flesh. Warm juices exploded into my mouth and dribbled down my bare chest. I felt like I was consuming the earth, drinking the sun, exhaling the raw materials of life itself.

I sat lizardlike on the slope of our white bulkhead, soaking up the sun, savoring the tomatoes, and watching the antics of pill bugs as they rolled into tiny, perfect spheres. I could not have been more in the present, more childlike, more attuned to the rhythms of the ever-changing universe . . .

"Biilllly."

My reverie was instantly broken. My family had arrived to partake, en masse, of their indoor, to my mind, far more pedestrian meal. They proceeded to argue and plan, bicker and gulp down great mouthfuls of politically incorrect consumables. I would never let on that I had just dined with the gods, been drunk with the very essence of the universe.

After breakfast the house filled with the drowsy heat of a mid-August day. Fat flies blundered into screen doors and a lone cicada scraped his strident song from a nearby pine. It would be time to get on with the real business of the day, exploration and investigation. My first chore was to catch grasshoppers to feed our resident box turtle. She was an old friend. I caught her every spring, fed her all summer, then marked and released her again in the fall. But she was a particularly finicky old friend who absolutely refused to eat anything easy to capture like earthworms or hamburger. She insisted, instead, on eating a daily ration of several dozen hard-to-catch live grasshoppers. So I had to spend several hours a day on hands and knees, searching for her delicacies. I grew adept at spying grasshoppers in the grass, and I can still remember the feeling of their taut little bodies as they struggled to get away.

After catching grasshoppers, it would be time to load up our old wooden-slated wheelbarrow with the tools of my trade: crab nets, fishing poles, clam rakes, and wire baskets—best to be prepared for any eventuality. I paused at a rickety old plank bridge that spanned a creek that emptied the marsh behind our house. I had to lie on the bridge in order to reach a piece of cod line tied to my minnow trap. As soon as the trap broke the surface it came alive with scores of thrashing, splashing fish. These were the dumb minnows that had moved in with last night's tide, not the resident fish who understood the dangers that lurked beneath the bridge. I pulled a few of the hapless minnows from the trap and plopped them into a bucket of seawater. They would come in handy if I came across some "snappers," young bluefish that had just moved into the bay from their offshore breeding grounds.

I finally reached the shore and hauled my flat-bottomed skiff into the bay. My father built the boat for skimming through the shallow creeks of the marshes behind the islands. Clamped firmly to the transom of the skiff was my pride and joy, a navy blue, three-horse Evinrude outboard. Brand loyalty was fierce on the bay. You either had an Evinrude or a Johnson, drove a Chevy or a Ford, or voted Democrat or Republican. My friends and I had long discussions about the merits of each.

I set the choke and pulled the cord. A cough, a sputter, a puff of blue smoke, and the battle was finally won. The motor caught and held a steady rhythm.

It was always easy to find my companions. We were the only ones on the bay at seven in the morning. Hank was on the far shore, Mayo was loading his boat for fishing, Stevie had just rounded Sprague Point, and Hobbs was puttering down Arey's River. Soon we would all collect in midbay and our daily discussion of tactics would ensue.

"Let's go catch some stripers."

"Nah, tide's all wrong. We'll never catch any."

"Menhaden are in. Saw some blues chasing 'em near Strong Island."

"Yeah, but the tide's goin' out. Let's look for some blue crabs."

Logic finally won the day. Fresh water flowed out of Lonnie's Pond at low tide. It was just strong enough to flush the turbidity of the salt water into the bay, so we could see the crabs lurking beneath large bright green mats of sea lettuce. We cut our engines and let the currents carry us downstream. Our eyes, trained from so much practice, knew how to ignore the crabs' greenish gray camouflage and look instead for patterns: the telltale edge of a crimson claw or the faint outline of a lurking carapace. We knew just how to plunge the net in front of the crab so it couldn't skitter to the side as it scuttled toward the safety of the overhanging bank. Once we had a crab in our bucket there was a mad scramble to to slam a board on top. You had to be quick. More than once we went home with fingers lacerated by the lightening quick slashes of a blue crab claw.

After an hour, the tide slowed and the water turned turbid again. The wind rustled the silvery undersides of poplars on Kent's Point and a school of menhaden circled just below the surface. Suddenly the school erupted into a thousand fusiform bodies. That was our cue. Snapper blues were hunting the menhaden from below. We hooked up some minnows and had soon caught half a dozen of the scrappy little fish.

The snappers always whetted our appetite for bigger game. This was a dangerous business. We would have to head down the bay to search for striped bass. But the Namequoit Sailing Association was in session and most of our parents were members. If we were not careful, they would shanghai us into crewing for one of their adult races— a fate worse than Latin class or dancing school. The only way such an experience could prove to be the least bit entertaining was if you happened to end up in the boat of one of the more articulate adults. Then you might pick up a salty new expression, or learn a risqué new term for a hitherto unmentionable piece of human anatomy. You might even hear guarded remarks about mysterious activities taking place between consenting adults. We always reported such educational tidbits to our group and spent long hours divining their intent and meaning.

But on most days we were able to happily elude our parents, hug the far shore, and scoot down the bay without losing any of our members. Our destination was the flats off faraway Crooked Channel, where the incoming tide swept silversides over the lip of the flats into deep holes where the schoolie bass lay in ambush. The calls of excited terns always drew us to the exact spot. The silversides were caught in a viscious crossfire, with terns diving unerringly from above and bass slashing viciously from below. By the end of the frenzy, the air was replete with the smell of fish oil and plankton and the water was full of fish scales, fluttering silvery down toward the bottom.

We fished furiously until the tide slowed and mats of drifting eelgrass started to foul our gear. Now it was time to head to the outer beach to dig some steamers and take a dip in the cold icy waters of the Atlantic. When we finished it was dead low tide, and we had to drag our boats across a hundred feet of dried-out flats.

But before long, we had enough water to play "ambush" in the acres of marsh behind the islands. While the other team counted, our team roared off in the labyrinth of creeks. Soon we were swallowed up in thick stands of marsh grass that towered over our heads. We maneuvered our boats into small creeks on either side of the main channel and waited. We felt like Athenian sailors waiting for Persian triremes to blunder into the straits of Messina, but we were probably more like Vietcong irregulars waiting to ambush American swiftboat captains. Now the second team of boats puttered slowly down the creek, searching for our positions.

"Shh, shh. Don't move. Don't move. Not now, not now."

The boats would putter on past to where the creek narrowed and they had to turn.

"Now, now! They're trapped. Get 'em, get 'em!"

"Hurry before they turn!"

"Fire! Fire!"

With all oars splashing, we blasted out of our side creeks with the sun at our sterns. It was glorious victory, but the conquered refused to submit. We settled the dispute with a long drawn-out water fight that left us all drenched, laughing, and almost swamped. We called a truce so we could pole back out to Sampson's Island, where we could clean and bail our soggy boats.

But when someone spotted a horseshoe crab, our play would become far less innocent. We became instantly transformed into a crazed bunch of little Ahabs launching our oars into the defenseless creatures.

Would this kid ever harm a horseshoe crab? *Photo by Jessie Sargent.*

I can still remember the satisfying crunch that a horseshoe crab shell makes when it receives a direct hit.

Such blood lust was sanctioned on Cape Cod in the fifties. Most towns still had bounties on horseshoe crabs because they were considered shellfish predators. Children were encouraged to capture any horseshoe crab they could find, wrench off its tail, and turn that in to the shellfish constable for a penny a tail. It was a mind set I spent years trying to overturn.

We motored quickly back up the bay in order to have enough light to clean the fish on the bridge above our creek. This was long work, slowed by impromptu anatomy lessons. I had to check out the stomach contents of each fish and fed select tidbits to my friends in the creek. I knew each minnow, crab, and shrimp as individuals and had given them names. "Black-back" lived under the bank, "Whitie" was submissive, and "Double-spot" was the first to steal bait from an adversary. I spent the last few hours of the day lying face down on the bridge, watching the behavior of my fascinating friends. My hunter-gatherer instincts had already started to evolve into more systematic study.

In fact, I have a private theory that such hunter-gatherer behavior is necessary to the development of true biological curiosity. If so, I fear that future scientists and doctors will miss out. They will never have the chance to discover nature for themselves, never have the chance to dissect a real organism.

I put my theory to the test whenever I elect to have minor surgery. I always go to my old friend Mayo Johnson, chief of surgery at the Beverly Hospital. I know he has a good technique, I watched him perfect it, filleting flounders on the rickety bridge above our creek.

The end of the summer was always a deeply sorrowful time. Family legend has it that one summer I was told quite precisely, "Now Billy, you can take your boat out for one last spin, but be sure to be back by nine o'clock sharp. We want to get an early start back to Dover."

I took out the boat, and one thing led to another, as they so often do on the water. There was one last crab to catch, one last creek to explore, and before I knew it, it was getting dark. It was well past sunset when I finally returned, to the consternation of my entire fuming family.

Winters were a long haul. I was a mediocre student who only expended effort when something piqued my own particular interests. I spent long dreary hours slogging through math and memorizing, by rote, list upon list of vocabulary words. The only time I exhibited a glimmer of potential was when my teacher gave us an assignment like, "Write about what you did last summer," "Describe a garden after a rain storm," or "Write about a snowy night." I would use these assignments to display my growing accumulation of scientific knowledge. My favorite books were already books like *Animals Without Backbones,* often used in college courses, and a graduate-level entomology textbook given to me by one of the scientists who worked for my father.

In the second grade my teacher asked our class to draw pictures of what we wanted to be when we grew up. Two of us wanted to be scientists, but what a difference between us. Sandy Archibald drew a picture of himself sitting alone at a workbench surrounded by glassware. I drew a picture of myself standing in front of a rapt audience of eager faces—a bit grandiose to be sure, but all in all, not a bad visual image of what science writing is really all about. But it would take me several decades to understand what the right side of my brain was trying to tell me.

There was another interesting quirk to my childhood schooling. Almost every year I received the improvement prize for math or English. This was not necessarily a good thing. It signaled, instead, that my teachers thought I was smart enough to know I could coast along all winter, then expend just enough effort to snag the improvement prize in the spring—in short it seemed to be a prize for laziness and connivance as much as for improvement.

A modern psychologist would probably call me disengaged and affectless in winter, and fully engaged if not hypomanic in the summer. These, in fact, are the diagnostic criteria used to diagnose seasonal affective disorder (SAD), an affliction that has shaped my life in innumerable ways. It is probably the main reason I write for a living, the reason I write about the things I write about, and, as we shall see, the reason I write the way I write.

One more incident clinches my diagnosis of early-onset seasonal affective disorder. One winter, my parents came down with the strange idea of spending Christmas in Florida. Now, you have to understand that the idea of spending Christmas lying on a beach in Florida was considered somewhat bohemian, if not downright disreputable, to someone from New England. You were supposed to stay at home, shovel snow, visit relatives, and ski on rocks and ice. This was character building. But to sit on beach and enjoy yourself? Sacrilege!

But my parents decided to buck convention. We all clambered into sleeper cars at the Route 128 train station outside of Boston and trundled on southward. I vaguely remembered being woken up to see the lights of New York City, then Washington, but what really impressed me was seeing my first palm tree. Trees were not even supposed to have leaves in winter, yet here were trees with fronds rustling erotically in the night air, and coconuts dangling suggestively from branchless trunks.

Presents were virtually nil that year, basically consisting of whatever my mother could scrounge up at the local five and ten cents store. But I remember them still: a cap gun I watched her slip into her bag so I wouldn't see it, and a pair of new white sneakers that made me feel like I could run like the wind. They must have been truly remarkable sneakers, because I heard several young boys enviously nagging their mothers to buy them new sneakers as I glided gracefully by.

My memories of other Christmases have melted into a fuzzy amalgam of gaudy decorations, presents I didn't really want, and Christmas trees that had to be chopped down and thrown out. But my memory of this one Christmas is still etched in vivid detail. I remember the bright greens of tropical vegetation, the intriguing new behaviors of pelicans and porpoises, the rustling of palms and hibiscus, but mostly I remember the light. To this day I still love and yearn for the tropics, where it is always summer.

Expanding Horizons (1954–1959)

"Mrs. Sargent, your son is all right but I'm afraid there has been some brain damage. All he's talking about is some nonsense about worms, crabs, and bugs."

"Oh, that's perfectly all right. All he ever does is talk some nonsense about worms, crabs, and bugs."—The Boston Children's Hospital, 1954

I also learned my first lessons about conservation on Pleasant Bay. My unwritten "rule of the creek" stated that I could occasionally harvest a single blue crab, but it had to be a male, and it could only be one crab at a time. I knew the crab would be missed and that it would take several weeks for another crab to reoccupy its empty niche.

But one day a troop of teenagers came swaggering up the shore, armed with buckets and nets. It was obvious they meant business. I was cordial, initially offering to show them where they could catch a particularly large male crab. But that was not enough. They marched on, two by two on either side of the creek, driving the hapless crabs between them. The animals didn't have a chance. After netting the crabs, the little Visigoths immobilized the crabs by smashing their shells, then continued the slaughter. By the end of the day, two dozen crabs lay dead or dying. "One-claw," "Blue-eye," and "Crabette" all lay with guts exposed, bleeding slowly into the marsh. The boys had killed every crab. The creek would not recover all summer. I trudged back to the house, feeling angry, sad, and violated.

9

The author (sitting far left) and cabinmates at the Big Spring Ranch in Colorado.

That evening I developed a headache, felt nauseous, and had diarrhea. I had to get out of bed several times to vomit and started feeling dehydrated and delirious. By the morning I had slipped into a coma.

The local doctor was summoned. He was an old-fashioned, family doctor, known more for his compassion than his hygiene. He always had a fat cigar clamped firmly between two voluptuously thick lips, and a rain of ashes fell continuously onto his ample paunch and into the pot of water he boiled to sterilize his instruments.

Dr. Gallagher returned for several days, but my fever never broke. I'm told he had tears in his eyes when he finally confronted my parents. "I'm terribly sorry, but there's nothing more I can do. You better get your son up to the Children's Hospital as fast as you can." I think I remember the ambulance, the sirens, and my parents driving behind us as we tore up Route 6, but perhaps I'm mistaken. At the Children's Hospital, doctors ran tests, took electroencephalograms, introduced antibiotics, and waited.

One nurse became particularly interested in my case and would often pop in to check on my condition. One day she greeted my mother at the door, "Oh, I'm so glad you're here. Your son just woke up a few minutes ago, but I'm afraid there's been some brain damage. All he's talking about is some nonsense about worms, crabs, and bugs."

My mother gave a great sigh of relief. "Oh thank goodness! No, no, he's perfectly all right. All he ever does is talk some nonsense about worms, crabs, and bugs!"

The upshot of the incident, from my point of view, was that my mother finally gave me the microscope that I had been nagging her about for years. The microscope expanded my horizons from the bridge down into the world of the microscopic. I spent long days collecting water samples from the creek and bay, from ponds, streams, and swamps. I collected horseshoe crab eggs and watched them develop and hatch, I scrutinized the proboscis of sand worms as they skewered their writhing prey. I turned the microscope inward to examine myself. I scraped cells from the inside of my cheek, blood I drew from my left index finger, and sperm I collected from . . . well, you know where.

I spent hours peering into these miniature new worlds and made sketches of their inhabitants in row upon row of spiral notebooks. I felt like I was visiting new planets or being transported back in time. Later, masks and snorkels allowed me to venture out further in the bay to explore the behavior of larger creatures. During these investigations, it was the visual and imaginative right-brained experiences that were paramount. I gained great intellectual and aesthetic pleasure from seeing these animals up close. It was also during this time that Jacques Cousteau started making his signature films about exploring the oceans and Walt Disney was making his more anthropomorphic films about nature. I devoured these, along with films like *The Lost World* (1925) that envisioned a world where dinosaurs still stalked our planet.

But it was the microscope that became my constant companion. The first thing I did when we arrived at the Cape each summer was to set up a laboratory in a nook in my bedroom. I spent hours boring holes into wooden shelves so I would have places to hang my test tubes. I rebuilt the lab wherever we moved—to Dover, to Washington, D.C., the Shenandoah Valley, and back to Boston again.

The author swings a lariat beneath the Grand Teton Mountains. *Photo by Jessie Sargent.*

Writing Naturally

We moved to Washington, D.C., in 1959 so my father could work on a commission established by President Eisenhower to make recommendations about new policies for national parks and forests. One of their recommendations was to create national seashores. These new types of parks had to have more flexible establishment policies, since so many people already lived within their confines. They also became particularly important because they were located closer to major centers of population than traditional national parks. The Cape Cod National Seashore established under President Kennedy in August 1961 would become a major influence on my later work.

When we moved to Washington, my parents were told that the thing to do was to send me to the St. Alban's School. St. Alban's was an old-line private school where students like Al Gore and I were supposed to go while our parents did their time in Washington. But I took one look at the school's dark Dickensian buildings squeezed into the urban center of Washington and turned them down flat. Instead, I ended up in the rolling hills of Maryland at the Landon School—a school whose campus was so beautiful that Lady Bird Johnson visited us every spring to open Landon's annual azalea show.

But my real life centered around the houses we rented outside Washington, D.C. The first was a cow farm in McLean, Virginia, the second was near the Potomac River, and the third was a log cabin in the Shenandoah Mountains. The cabin was made from logs we cut on our land at the base of Old Rag Mountain. The one-room building had no electricity, no running water, and a working outhouse. Every morning I had to hike to a watercress-surrounded spring to retrieve several buckets of water for drinking and bathing.

Our nearest neighbor lived off the land. On any day of the week you could see a freshly killed bear, deer, or raccoon hanging from Archie's barn. He paid little attention to hunting seasons and showed me the locations of several mountain stills. He taught me how to catch turtles and how to flick live bait off your hook just before being apprehended by a park ranger. It was illegal to use the live caddis-fly larvae we found attached to rocks in the swiftly flowing streams.

Another neighbor lived with a pack of twenty dogs. The dogs took care of him, carefully nipping off any ticks the old man happened to pick up during the day. I understand that scientists are now using dogs to sniff out cancer cells. I'll bet Old Rob's dogs removed some of his cancerous skin lesions before they became malignant.

But most of my outdoor adventures occurred in McLean. Like most boys, I dreamed of building a raft and drifting down a river. The Potomac beckoned. A group of us cut down several sizable trees and nailed them together with lumber we stole from a nearby construction site. We hadn't taken into account that we had built the raft upstream of a six-foot dam. Fortunately, the trees we used were green so that when we launched the raft it was so waterlogged that it couldn't float over the dam and down into the treacherous rapids below.

Other adventures were more germane to the Washington area. One of my favorite pastimes was to walk our dogs around the site of the new CIA center under construction in the nearby Virginia woods. The site was surrounded with a twenty-foot-high chain link fence. All the culverts leading into the building were covered with heavy metal bars. But one day I looked up, and to my horror realized that my dog had somehow managed to crawl through a hole in the fence and was trotting along happily beside me.

Then all hell broke loose. Lights flashed, sirens sounded, and a jeep bristling with guns bore down upon us. A grim-faced soldier pointed a mounted machine gun at my dog and informed me he was trespassing on government property. It's a little difficult to try to convince your dog to crawl back through a small hole in a fence when a machine gun is trained at your head and your dog thinks this is the most fun he has had in years.

Another incident affected my natural history explorations more directly. For years I made a habit of collecting snakes. These were mostly small ring-necked snakes that crawled out of our houseplant pots when my mother brought them in for the winter. My pets did little to endear me to the rest of the family.

But on one particular day I was trotting down a steep path that led toward the Potomac River. The path was covered with leaves and strewn with loose boulders. Just before I put my foot down, I recognized the outline of a large copperhead snake lying on a bed of dried beech leaves. Perhaps all my years spent training my eyes to ignore the camouflage and look for the pattern of blue crabs had saved me. I was able to keep my balance just long enough to withdraw my foot before the copperhead awoke. My friends then dropped several large boulders on the coiled snake. I was too shaken to participate, and even after the copperhead was clearly dead, I could not bring myself to touch its five-foot length. In that one instant, I had gone from having a fascination with snakes to having a fear of them.

The same thing happened to my daughter with spiders. When she was a toddler she was fascinated with balls of lint that she called "rugkicks." But one day a piece of lint attached to a "rugkick" got caught in her trousers so that every time she moved the "rugkick" would appear to jump up after her. From that day on, she harbored a morbid fear of spiders.

A modern psychologist would argue that for most of our existence, humans have lived in small, open hunter-gatherer communities where spiders and snakes were common and deadly. When snakes slither through such communities today, modern hunter-gatherers grab their children and chase the snakes away, displaying both fear and fascination. Our distant primate relatives the vervet monkeys have specific calls for their three main enemies: snakes, eagles, and leopards, which all require different escape strategies. It would certainly not do for human children to retain an innate curiosity about a black mambo or cobra; on the other hand, it would certainly not be adaptive for a human child to lack curiosity altogether. Instead, humans have inherited a propensity to fear snakes and spiders. All it takes is one memorable encounter to trigger this fear, which can then last a lifetime. The younger this imprinting happens, the more long-lasting and powerful is the effect. I still like snakes and take photos of them from a distance, but the ancient phobia still niggles at the base of my brain.

Washington offered other inducements to my growing interest in science. My mother would drop me off at the edge of the city and I would spend days exploring the city's broad avenues and quirky back streets. I particularly loved the city's many and varied museums. One day I noticed a small bronze plaque on a building designating it as the Army Medical Museum. The guard at the door wasn't too comfortable admitting someone my age, but we couldn't find any regulation against it, so he let me in.

What a museum it turned out to be. There were no Disneylike exhibits and graphics aimed at the reading level of a twelve-year-old.

The museum existed for the professional use of surgeons, patholo-
gists, and forensic students. It had been established during the Civil
War to collect specimens of morbid anatomy. Acquisitions were easy.
The War Department simply sent out a directive to all its military surgeons, urging them to send in any interesting samples of their work.
One doctor sent in "Barnum's hip," showing where his patient, Barnum, had used ever-decreasing sizes of oakum cord to staunch a long-
lasting open belly bullet wound. Major General Sickles had sent his
own dismembered leg, and was said to visit the museum every year to
visit the missing member on the anniversary of its amputation.

Another huge swollen leg stood upright in a jar of formaldehyde. I
diagnosed the cause instantly. The swelling was from the filaria parasite that causes elephantiasis. I recognized the symptoms from my
obsessive rereadings of *Animals Without Backbones*. Another case exhibited the vertebrae of John Wilkes Booth, who had been shot in the
neck while holed up in a dirty barn in Virginia after assassinating
President Lincoln. "President Garfield's Vertebrae" were exhibited
nearby. Garfield had died not from the assassin's bullet still lodged
in his spine, but because the doctor searching for the bullet had not
washed his hands.

The exhibits went on. Feet with six toes, photos depicting the erad-
ication of yellow fever, a chainsaw used to speed up amputation before
the era of anesthesia, rows upon rows of jars filled with malformed
embryos and "Trichobezoan," the world's largest hairball removed
from the stomach of a twelve-year-old girl who obsessively ate her
own hair.

Far from horrifying me, the exhibits elicited a kind of professional
pride. I realized that my fascination with watching animals like the
parasite filaria under a microscope could lead to lifesaving discoveries. Other children with similar interests had gone on to eradicate diseases like elephantiasis in Africa and yellow fever in Panama. I felt like
I had been inducted into a professional place, made all the more fascinating because I had discovered it on my own.

On another evening I attended a more conventional lecture at the
National Geographic Society. Dr. Louis Leakey had just flown in from
Africa and told us about his recent excavations. At the conclusion of
his talk he casually reached into his jacket pocket and pulled out the

tooth of a million-year-old hominid that he had unearthed just a few days before. Now, there was a man who knew something about scientific showmanship.

Of course, you often bumped into famous people in Washington. We lived near Stuart Udall. The Secretary of the Interior was a Mormon and had a large, rambunctious family. I used to marvel at him talking on the phone to President Kennedy while several of his kids crawled in and out of his lap.

It snowed on the day President Kennedy was inaugurated. The Udalls called because they couldn't get their car out of the driveway. We gave them a lift and watched the inaugural from the Secretary's box. I still remember one of the invited dignitaries getting up to hold his hat over Robert Frost's fluttering pages so the great New England poet could recite his lines on that sparkling bright day.

The Udalls were a fun-loving lot. I was friends with several of the boys. I remember one Sunday morning we were skipping along the C&O Canal while our fathers were locked in deep conversation far behind us. We ran ahead and used our fingers to make fake deer tracks in the path. In no time at all, two of the top environmentalists in the country were down on their hands and knees examining the phony tracks.

"Hey, look here. Fresh deer tracks."

"Must have just gone by."

"Wonder where they are now?"

We let the two get in deeper and deeper until we finally admitted to our deception. Where was a *Life* photographer when you really needed one?

Adolescent Senescence (1960–1965)

During the three short years we were in Washington I was a largely unconscious observer, as the Eisenhower era and the fifties gave way to the Kennedy era and the sixties.

A major part of President Eisenhower's legacy was the speech he gave when leaving office. In it, this four-star general warned the nation about the dangers of the military-industrial complex. I saw the effects of the growing federal bureaucracy in the rural areas of Maryland and

Virginia. When we moved to McLean, Virginia, there was still an open-water ford in the center of town and I was able to ramble through thousands of acres of undisturbed fields and forests. Three years later, most of that land had been converted to tract homes and office parks. Money was flowing into the area to support the military-industrial complex and the network of private companies that help support it. Washington was becoming the center of a new empire. Successful families from all over America, indeed the world, were converging on Washington. Many found the city so congenial they stayed long after their government service had ended. The city was being transformed from the national equivalent of a sleepy state capitol to a glittering center of power, if not culture.

Of course, most of this meant very little to me at the time. I do remember being petrified when I first learned that we would be going to Washington. It was the era when we were taught to dive under our school desks in the event of a nuclear war, and I figured Washington would be the first city to be attacked. Evidently many of our neighbors felt the same way; three of them had built well-stocked bomb shelters on our short ten-block street. Several times a year wave upon wave of helicopters flew over our house. It was a drill; they were ferrying all the members of Congress, the White House, and the Cabinet to top-secret bunkers buried beneath the mountains of rural Virginia.

Washington also harbored the flavor of the pre-Civil Rights south. In 1959 I remember watching a confused and flustered young white waitress break into tears and run into the kitchen of a local restaurant, saying she couldn't serve a black family. The manager came out and politely explained the situation and asked the black family to leave. I felt agony for the mortified family as they quietly left the restaurant. How would the parents explain the situation to their son and daughter, dressed in their Sunday best? But mostly I felt furious with myself and the adults I was with, for sitting there stunned as the unfortunate scene unfolded. I had never witnessed such blatant discrimination, but I would soon be going back to Boston where the discrimination was just as cruel, only more institutionalized and better hidden from view. I had never spoken to a black person in Boston. At least in Washington I had become friends with Willie, an elderly black man who taught me how to catch spring shad in the swollen Potomac River. This would have never happened in the Boston of the early sixties.

But these were mostly exciting, heady years in Washington, D.C. Every Christmas I sang at the White House and the National Art Museum with the Landon School choir. I hobnobbed with the sons and daughters of senators, congressmen, and the press. It was only at later college reunions that I discovered that several of their "State Department dads" had actually been CIA operatives. Their children had only learned about their fathers' work in their adult years, though they had often wondered why foreign governments always seemed to crumble immediately after their fathers had been posted there.

It was with some reluctance that our family moved back to Boston. But for me, the move was made easier because I couldn't wait to get my hands on the big microscopes at my new high school. I envisioned spending long afternoons doing my own research under the watchful eye of a trusted mentor. But that was not to be. The school's lone biology teacher had been hired more to coach the varsity football team than to teach biology to a bunch of sophomores. We often hear about those wonderful teachers who help students discover their life's work, but how often do we hear about those bored and boring teachers who turn students away from their rightful paths?

Still, it wasn't all my teacher's fault that I turned away from my natural interest in biology. For me, attending the Noble and Greenough school was like returning home. I knew several of my classmates from previous schools and they made me feel instantly welcome. I was no longer an outsider and the new kid at school. Nobles, at that time, was an eclectic mixture of an all boys private boarding school and a local day school. About a third of us were five-day boarders, but we thought of ourselves as the core of the school.

The essence of a boarding school lies in the requirement that it must keep its students occupied and out of trouble 24 hours a day. Athletic events and homework left me with little time for any private interests, let alone independent research. My biophilia and laboratory lay sadly idle.

I was also pulled toward other things. My roommate Rick Railsback was a natural leader, one of the most popular kids in the class, and a bit of an imp. Rick took me under his wing, and by proxy I fell in with a faster crowd than I would have found on my own. The experience made me more gregarious than had I followed my own, more naturally introverted inclinations.

One warm night in the spring of our senior year, Rick convinced me to go swimming at an outside pool about a quarter of a mile from our dorm. We slipped out of our room and down to the pool but became lost on our return. Our dormitory was a castle that had been built by an eccentric old businessman who was said to have made much of his fortune by smuggling liquor during Prohibition. An underground passage that led from the Charles River to the castle lent some credence to the stories. His castle was also riddled with numerous secret passageways and winding back stairs. We got lost in several of these dark passageways while trying to return undetected to our room. Finally we found it and prepared to slip quietly into bed. But suddenly there was a cry: "Benny? Benny! There's someone in our room." We recognized the voice instantly. We had somehow blundered into the bedroom of the strictest teacher on campus. We ran out the door and down the stairs with Ben Lawson in hot pursuit. We finally found our way outside and flattened ourselves up against the castle wall. A flashlight beam danced fitfully along the wall until it finally caught us, dripping, stark naked, and terrified. I don't know who gave the greater sigh of relief when Mr. Lawson finally recognized us. As I remember it, we didn't get into too much trouble because we looked so ridiculous and had been proved to be so comically inept.

While science took a backseat during my adolescence, writing became more important. An alumnus wrote a stuffy article about his pride in working for President Johnson and supporting the war in Vietnam. I wrote back a cheeky letter, which caught the attention of the faculty advisor of our school newspaper. He asked me to write a weekly column that allowed me to poke gentle fun at school life and the world in general. In our junior year, a Boston radio station asked our class to take part in a debate about the Vietnam War. This was in 1964, before opposition to the war had really started to coalesce. I was up against one of the smartest kids in our class who was staunchly in favor of the war. I marshaled my arguments and likened the United States to the Sheriff of Nottingham and Ho Chi Minh to Robin Hood. I won the debate mostly on the basis of such cheap shots and realized I liked the audience. It was a little bit like being back in that second-grade drawing of what I wanted to be when I grew up . . . only missing the science.

Perhaps the most memorable experience of my high school career was writing a play for our senior class. The play was a takeoff on Romeo and Juliet, centering the story on the rivalry between our school and that of our arch-enemy, Milton Academy. The idea came to me one spring night, and I wrote most of the play in the following weeks. Our school had never staged a student-written play nor held one that included the entire senior class. I had to get special permission from the headmaster, who conveniently decided to go away for that weekend. The play was held on a Saturday night, the audience roared, and we even made a fair amount of money.

Today, one of the first rules I try to drill into my students is, "Show, don't tell." It means don't just blurt out "This is important" or "Joe was nervous"; instead, write, "Joe fiddled with the hem of his well-worn jacket." The next thing I tell them is, "Don't pay any attention to rules. Writing is an art, not a science. Use your own judgment." This is one of those times when it is necessary to break the the first rule. Writing my senior play was important.

It was important, not because the play was particularly well written, nor because it was such an original idea to place Romeo and Juliet in a modern setting—remember *West Side Story?* No, the play was noteworthy because it is a perfect example of what I mean by writing naturally. Researchers have found that most writers have varying degrees of seasonal affective disorder, and many do 80 percent of their work during the spring and summer months. It is then that the amount of daylight is changing the most, when ideas mix fast and furiously, and when you have increased energy and enthusiasm. You are caught in the intoxicating grip of hypomania, a speedy kind of euphoria set slightly above normal but slightly under the hypermania of the truly bipolar. It was this hypomania that gave me the unrealistic confidence that the play couldn't possibly fail. Of course, it wasn't all easy; nobody showed up for the first rehearsal. But eventually we pulled it all together. Some people helped with writing, others with direction, lights, a live band, and sound. All of us discovered we had talents we never knew we possessed. This was amazing both to us and to the rest of the school. We were the vanguard of the sixties, and the faculty considered our class to be full of long-haired rebels, so unlike the more tractable students who had come before us.

The important thing was that we wrote the play for our own amusement, bonded together as outcasts do, and managed to fill an entire auditorium with laughter at our faculty's expense.

Personally, I tasted the sweet power of subversive writing and wanted more. The play was a little like the drawing of what I wanted to be when I grew up, but without the science. But science could take a backseat. I felt I had found my métier. It would become a familiar seesaw, switching back and forth between writing and science. It would take me several more years to discover that I didn't really have to choose. I could end up doing both.

Of course, there was one more aspect to my adolescent years. During my early years in high school I often joined my friends taking girls on dates where we groped, rather unsuccessfully as I remember it, at various drive-in movies. That changed when my mother met a young French girl flying to Boston to study English and be an au pair. My mother invited Claudie to our house for several weekends, and soon I was deeply in love. It was not difficult. Claudie was beautiful, several years older, and many years more sophisticated than I. I don't know what my parents were thinking. We lived in a contemporary house that my father had designed. All the rooms were strung out in a long line on a single floor. I had never really appreciated the design until Claudie and I discovered how easy it was to get together at night undetected. For most of my senior year we lived together, every weekend, as man and wife. I can't think of a better way to be introduced to the intricacies of love, sex, and commitment. After that, I held my counsel, whenever my friends started to relate stories about their latest conquest at the drive-in movies.

I know I benefited from falling so deeply in love during my adolescent years. It was a little like being imprinted with a template for future relationships. At the risk of being considered hopelessly out-of-date, I wonder about the emotional repercussions of today's emphasis on "hooking up" and having "friends with benefits," even though it is a somewhat logical response to the threat of AIDS and other sexually transmitted diseases.

I now know a neuroscientist who teaches that during adolescence, our brain is being so bombarded with hormones and is so preoccupied with guiding our sexual development that its rational areas simply go into a kind of early senescence. He argues that it would really be better if we just took a few years off during those turbulent years to concentrate solely on sex and bonding. I doubt his ideas will really catch on, but I think anyone who has ever been through adolescence will know what he is getting at. So with all those same hormones juicing through my system, it was an astonishment to both me and many other people that I did reasonably well on my SATs and was accepted into college, where my life would really begin.

Chapter 2

College

Observing the Molecular Wars: My Early College Years (1965–1967)

I arrived at Harvard College as a callow undergraduate, wondering if I would ever find anything I was particularly good at doing. There always seemed to be someone down the hall who had just written a book, produced a play, or been picked up by a major recording label.

The summer before my freshman year, I read *On Aggression* and *The Territorial Imperative,* two books that used research on animal behavior to say powerful things about evolution and human nature. That was the path I wanted to pursue, but I didn't see how I could study such things in the traditional undergraduate biological curriculum. So instead, I decided to major in government. It seemed like the obvious thing to do. My father had been elected lieutenant governor of Massachusetts in 1965, and going into government service seemed to be a lot like going into the family business—a bit of a tradition in Massachusetts politics.

One of my roommates had a friend who had been selected to take a freshmen seminar at Harvard's Museum of Comparative Zoology. One day he invited us to have lunch in the museum's malacology department, where he was helping to catalogue their extensive collection of mollusks. We entered the department by going through a basement side door, where we were instantly surrounded by huge plaster casts of dinosaur tracks and assailed by the heady smell of formaldehyde. To this day, that smell stirs my imagination and remains intimately linked to an intellectual awakening.

A painting of the famous geologist Louis Agassiz glowered down upon us. Did he deem us qualified to undertake the painstaking task of gathering knowledge to pass on to future generations? Doubtful! I followed my friend down an aisle between a hippopotamus and two lion cubs, preserved forever in glass cases. We mounted a wrought iron staircase beside a gorilla beating his breast, passed beneath the skeleton of a sperm whale, and rang the bell of the malacology department.

A white coated scientist gave us a jovial greeting, then led us between more wooden shelves to the inner sanctum itself. I felt like I was Alice in Wonderland being presented at the Mad Hatter's Tea Party. Seated around the table, brown bag lunches spread out before them, were people who shared the same odd passions as myself. They had studied nature and traveled the world; they could answer my questions and understand my passions.

I had stumbled into the very midst of the intellectual life I had been seeking. But no one took particular notice of my excitement; the group was locked in one of its famous discussions. Loud, boisterous, witty, and opinionated, the arguments swung wildly from the role of deodorants in the ruination of America's sex life, to politics, to collecting snails in pre-Castro Cuba.

An odd-looking Welshman seemed to be in command. He sat at the head of the table, probing, questioning, adding insights, and relating a long story complete with sound effects about duck hunting in Wales. Someone made a point and Ken Read's deep rich resonant Welsh baritone boomed out over the already high decibel level: "Good God, you know, you might be right!" It was followed by his instantly infectious staccato laugh. Ruth Turner chimed in with a story about collecting shipworms from old wooden wrecks in the Indian Ocean. George Buckley posed a question about color variation in the opercula of distant Tineids. He had been cataloging the museum's collection of mollusks from his earliest days in high school. Ken Read was professor of biology at Boston University who would become one of the pioneers of underwater photography, and Ruth Turner was an adventurous scientist who had a Navy grant to study shipworms. Little did I know how much each of these people would shape my life forever.

Now I had a dilemma. The experience made me realize that I had always harbored an inborn love of nature. To tell the truth, it seemed horribly unfair that my roommate's friend had been admitted to his freshman seminar solely on the basis of his good grades, not because he had any particular interest in mollusks or nature! Even though it would entail slogging through four years of math, plus inorganic and organic chemistry, I realized I had to major in biology. It would mean I would have little time to write, but the rewards seemed worth it.

I plunged ahead in my sophomore year, taking introductory biology, invertebrate zoology, and a tutorial on the chemistry and structure of hemoglobin. Bio 1A was taught in the grand manner by the avuncular George Wald, who would soon go on to win the Nobel Prize. My house tutor was to become a well-known activist and researcher on HIV and AIDS, but my obsession was invertebrate zoology. I was back in my lab, peering happily though the microscope and making detailed drawings. The course had an old-fashioned feel that I enjoyed. Our professor was an arachnidologist whose notes were so old that flecks of them would flutter to the floor when he opened his folder to lecture. The graduate students teaching our labs knew the names of each specimen's appendage but seemed never to have seen the animals living in the field. I had grown up with most of the creatures and knew about their behaviors in intimate detail. But it didn't really matter; we spent our Saturdays on field trips and in the lab. We taught our professor's trap-door spiders to leap out menacingly at any unsuspecting visitor roaming down the halls. We fancied ourselves as the intelligentsia, diligently studying nature while our less perceptive classmates spent their weekends attending football games. I was thrilled to be back in my lab studying worms, crabs, and bugs.

As an undergraduate, however, I was only vaguely aware that the biology department was going through a major coup. The molecular biologists had declared holy war on traditional biology. They were convinced that studying biology on the molecular level was the wave of the future and that systematics, ecology, behavior, and the study of whole animals amounted to little more than stamp collecting. They were determined to win the war by purging the department of whole-animal biologists and of courses in such old-fashioned crusty old subjects as invertebrate zoology and animal behavior. But I was just discovering that I liked the musty old corners of science. Such eccentricities might be all right for a writer, but it could be professional suicide for an ambitious young scientist!

The molecularists were led by James Watson, the co-discoverer of the structure of DNA and one of the youngest men to ever win the Nobel Prize. The prize was said to further inflate his already over-inflated ego. Watson was an intellectual conquistador who boasted in *The Double Helix* that he and Francis Crick were so brilliant that that they didn't have to do any of the laborious bench work normally done by biologists. They had just "noodled some ideas about in their heads" until their earthshaking discovery had emerged. No one had anticipated such a rapid discovery. It was as if an alien had swooped down out of the sky and given us the key to understanding life without our having to do any of the hard work—hard work from which wisdom often arises.

Watson had adopted a brusque and swaggering air irresistible to undergraduates and widely copied by his fellow graduate students. We watched as one of our Radcliffe classmates started out in the back of one of his seminars, then inched up class by class until the end of our junior year, when she married the dashing young teacher. How could we compete with a recent graduate student who had just won the Nobel Prize and written one of the best science books ever published?

Watson's acolytes considered themselves to be the wave of the future, the young Turks who would purge the department of courses like invertebrate zoology—studying whole animals was no longer necessary, they were simply "black boxes" that housed the all important DNA. I still know scientists who can tell you everything about a crab's neuron, but nothing about how that neuron affects the animal's behavior. The traditional roles of whole-animal biologists were to classify an animal and to determine how it behaved and interacted with other animals in the environment. Scientists who pursued these careers were the systematists, behaviorists, and ecologists that molecular biologists wanted to eradicate.

Of course, the molecular biologists were onto something. The discovery of the structure of DNA had unleashed biotechnology and with it the key to eradicating disease and feeding the world's hungry. It was crucially important to develop techniques to splice and replicate genes. But what about the knowledge that could be derived from ecology to counter the rapid destruction of the natural world? What about the insight derived from animal behavior to explain how difficult it would be to change human nature? Even though environmental awareness was on the horizon, the molecularists were waging a war to get rid of the very subjects that would inform that awareness the most. But what good were insight and wisdom against the power, profit, and glory that could be made from molecular biology?

Watson and his followers were opposed by a traditional biologist who memorably described Watson as the Caligula of modern biology. E. O. Wilson was a journeyman field biologist who had spent much of his career humbly deciphering the systematics and behavior of ants. It was a controversy over both style and substance. As an undergraduate I was only vaguely aware of the vitriol flying overhead, but the controversy would be one I would observe and write about for the rest of my life.

Meanwhile, I was having my own problems. I didn't think I had the single-minded determination to stay up all night memorizing the structure of each molecule of hemoglobin, a subject that is so complex that creationists now wrongly use it as evidence for intelligent design!

There were just too many other courses I wanted to take and experiences I wanted to enjoy. I was also in love with Judy Friedlaender, a fellow undergraduate at Radcliffe. During vacations we would drive down to New York to visit with her engaging family. Her father had season tickets to the Metropolitan Opera and took us there faithfully. He also invited me to their synagogue, the oldest and most prestigious in New York City. I had been brought up to think that arriving on the *Mayflower* was pretty hot stuff. These were heady discoveries for a provincial young kid from Boston!

By my sophomore year, I was also being considered for acceptance in one of Harvard's social clubs. I'm embarrassed to admit how important it seemed at the time. We were wined and dined at various estates on the North and South Shores. The underlying message of the punching season was that it wasn't really very important how you did in academics; what was essential was to line up contacts for a future in the cozy confines of Boston's legal and business professions. I didn't know exactly what I did want to do, but I knew I damn well didn't want that. Besides, it was winter. I was depressed and convinced I had spent so much time on invertebrate zoology that I could never pass my other courses. It was a little like one of those anxiety dreams where you discover you are supposed to take an exam for a course you never attended, only this wasn't a dream, it was real.

Happily, Ruth Turner stepped into this confusion. She knew a Woods Hole scientist who needed someone to collect plankton on a six-month cruise to South America, Africa and the Baltic. I would be back working with worms, crabs, and bugs, but on a grand scale. I had to get permission from my parents and sit down with my local draft board and agree to join Harvard's controversial ROTC Naval Reserve Officers Corps on my return to college. It seemed like a small price to pay for having the chance to participate in such a fascinating adventure.

The Atlantis II *(1967)*

The veliger's a lively tar, the liveliest afloat,
A whirling wheel on either side propels his little boat.
—Walter Garstang, *Larval Forms and*
Other Zoological Verses, 1951

It is January 6, 1967. Big, fat flakes of snow swirl out of the inky sky, dance silver in the beam of the overhead light, then die quietly in the hissing black waters of the Atlantic. I am standing on the bow of the *Atlantis II* wondering what the next six months will bring. Did Charles Darwin feel this way as he watched the White Cliffs of Dover slip quietly astern? What are my classmates doing as they prepare for the second half of their sophomore year?

Our work begins as the ship heaves to at midnight. Rudi Scheltema inches out on a narrow platform high above the rolling deck. Captain Hiller's voice come over the squawk box:

"We have zero headway. You boys ready to set the net?"

"Affirmative. Net going over."

Rudi gives a thumbs-up and I drop the tail of the fifteen-foot net into the roiling waters. The winchman releases a lever and the net sinks quickly below the waves. It is important to lower the net quickly so the ship won't drift over its trawl wire.

"Bridge, what's our speed and course, over?"

"Two knots, 213 degrees. Do you read, over?"

"Affirmative. Two knots 213 degrees. Got that, over and out."

The net is now swimming at an 18-degree angle behind us. The

The author has coffee with his parents and Dr. Paul Fye before departing on a six-month cruise to Africa, South America, and the Baltic aboard the R/V *Atlantis II*. *Courtesy of the* Boston Globe.

bridge will keep it fishing at a hundred meter depth while we prep the midships lab.

Half an hour later we record the trawl data and carry the sample below for sorting and identification. Rudi loaned me a copy of Sir Alister Hardy's classic book *The Open Ocean* a month before the cruise. It is filled with watercolors of plankton Hardy made on the decks of British Fisheries vessels while the creatures were still alive. Still, I am unprepared for the exquisite forms and flamboyant colors of the tiny living creatures. A ciliated velum keeps the veligers afloat, and tiny black eyes give them a comical air. For the next two hours we sit glued to our eyepieces, separating the plankton by genus and species.

This was my daily chore every noon and midnight for the next six months, and I never tired of the deeply satisfying aesthetic experience. Rudi was in the process of discovering that populations of bottom-living mollusks on the eastern and western sides of the Atlantic are

The author demonstrates a bathythermograph to Vice-President Hubert Humphrey on a show-and-tell cruise aboard the R/V *Atlantis II*. *Courtesy of the* Boston Globe.

related. The question was, how did they get there? We were beginning to see that one generation of adults living in the shallow waters off of Africa releases its young as plankton. The plankton are then entrained into the great gyre of currents that drift clockwise around the North Atlantic Ocean. When these larval forms reach the American coast, they develop quickly and settle out as bottom-living adults. The following generation reverses the process. The tiny larval wisps of protoplasm have to be able to correctly detect the odor of the correct substrate in order to successfully complete their life cycles. Rudi had to teach me the ropes quickly. He would leave the ship in Bermuda and I would be on my own for the next six months.

A few days later, a squall line appeared on the distant horizon. We were still in the North Atlantic, but we could see the sun shining on the other side of the storms. A distinct line separated the deep green waters of the Atlantic from the turquoise blue of the Gulf Stream. As soon as our bow crossed the line the sun came out and the temperature soared into the eighties. It would stay there for the next six months.

The ship then settled into a comfortable routine. We read, ate, collected data, and got to know our fellow shipmates. Rudi and I made plankton tows every noon and midnight and helped the benthic biologists collect bottom samples. It was always a shock to plunge your hands into the light gray siliceous mud. Even on the hottest days, it was only a few degrees above freezing. We would sit on deck, happily chatting about biological minutia while sifting through the mud looking for long-legged pycnygonid sea spiders and iridescent, twisting, pink polychaete worms.

Howie Saunders was recording the relative paucity of animals in the deep-sea abyssobenthic ocean. Little did I know that a few years later I would watch him on television whooping with joy as he pulled eight-foot-long, blood-red vestimentiferan worms out of pressurized canisters. He would be one of the first people to see and describe the new communities of animals found thriving in the dark in the superheated waters boiling out of the earth's interior. Up until that time, everyone thought all life depended on food derived from photosynthesis. Yet here were ancient communities receiving all their energy from the chemosynthesis of sulfur boiling out of the deep-sea vents that line the world's system of globe-girdling mid-oceanic rifts. The discovery would revolutionize biology, vindicate the theory of continental drift, and prepare us to examine life on other planets.

The plankton communities changed as we entered the Gulf Stream. The teeming masses of copepods gave way to the less numerous but more exotic tropical species. One day we hauled in a clump of sargassum weed that seemed to be bound together by a gelatinous piece of monofilament. No one could identify the curious specimen. A few days later I was in the ship's library thumbing through the log of the *HMS Challenger,* the British research vessel whose 1870s round-the-world cruise had launched the study of oceanography. The *Challenger* scientists had also collected plankton in these waters. I looked at the book's exquisite color plates and there it was, the same specimen we had captured a few days before. They had correctly identified what looked like monofilament as the long stringy egg masses of the sargassum fish—a hundred years before us. Another volume showed Ben Franklin's 1786 chart of the Gulf Stream, "the mighty river within a river" that he convinced American sailors to use to speed their passage across the Atlantic to deliver the mail. We were part of a continuum of scientists slowly dissecting the ocean's secrets.

On moonless nights I would often take a mattress and climb down to the bow observation chamber three decks below. The chamber was a sort of bulbous supernumerary nose located six feet below the ship's waterline. I could lie back on my mattress in the cramped chamber and watch plankton shoot by an array of five strategically placed portholes. Millions of gelatinous creatures would appear out of the gloom, flash bluish green beside us, then disappear quickly astern. Occasionally a larger creature would flash a fist-sized orb of annoyance. It was like driving through a blizzard of bioluminescence.

Suddenly I heard a chorus of whistles and the entire chamber lit up. A pod of dolphins had joined us and they were swimming on the other side of the thin hull. I could hear their calls only inches from my ears. I could see their eyes staring at me through the portholes. Contrails of bioluminescence twisted off their tail flukes as they drove on beside us. Occasionally a dolphin would veer off to the side, then return to resume its station. This would be accompanied with excited bursts of clicks and whistles.

I climbed back up to the main deck to see if I could discover what was going on. From the bow, I could look directly down on the blazing bodies of the rapidly swimming dolphins as they drove through the sea of plankton. But suddenly there was a silent explosion up ahead and a dozen nine-inch-long projectiles shot to either side of our oncoming bow. They were squid that looked like roman candles as they streaked through the bioluminescent waters. Then I understood it. The dolphins were veering off like fiery torpedoes to catch and consume the squid. It was the equivalent of a dolphin drive-by shooting.

After a few days, we reached Bermuda. Actually, we smelled the odor of her vegetation before we actually saw the island. British sailors used to say they could smell Bermuda's onions before they caught sight of the land. It was my first experience slipping into a tropical port.

Everything was business in the St. George's Harbor. We had to off-load biological specimens and break out chemical equipment for the next leg of the cruise. But I did have time to join a group of scientists walking through the Bermuda Botanical Gardens. This was where John Lennon spotted the double fantasy plant that gave its name to the *Double Fantasy* album, which would prove to contain the last recordings of one of our era's great balladeers. Frankly, I was more enchanted by the group of oceanographers reciting the Latin names of each tropical plant and flower, to the delight of their companions. This was the scientific equivalent of reciting poetry, a tad pretentious perhaps, but satisfying nonetheless. These were the same species I had fallen in love with in Florida, and now I was appreciating them with people who shared my fascination. Did I envy my classmates slogging through the slush and snow of Cambridge?

From Bermuda we proceeded to Dakar, Senegal, where a dozen eleven-foot manta rays led us into the harbor. In port we had to prepare for the next geological leg of our cruise, which would require new methods and equipment. The *Atlantis II* was the first civilian ship to carry an onboard computer. The refrigerator-sized machine could triangulate signals from three military satellites orbiting silently overhead. But the highly classified computer sat in the corner unused. Nobody trusted it. Today a child can use a similar hand-held GPS Global Positioning Satellite System to navigate his or her way to the nearest mall.

Excitement grew as we approached the mid-Atlantic ridge. We towed magnetometers, used thermisters to measure heat rising from beneath the ocean floor, and collected fifteen-foot cores of bottom mud. A sonar device bounced sound signals off the ocean bottom and back up to the ship. The scientific crew was in charge of recording the incoming signals on a continuously unwinding spool of graph paper. It was our job to keep the massive depth recorder calibrated so we wouldn't lose the bottom trace. This was easy above the abyssal plains, but once you approached the mid-Atlantic ridge the bottom rose dramatically, then descended back into the rift valley and then rose quickly back up again to the other side.

Our greatest fear was that we would doze off and lose the bottom trace, an easy thing to do when you were alone at the end of a 4 A.M. watch. You would wake with a start and have to madly scroll up and down and reset the scale until you recovered the bottom again. If you screwed up, you could be sure that the next watch would make all kinds of nasty notations on your section of the steadily unwinding graph. Nobody wanted to be known as the guy who lost the mid-Atlantic ridge.

But we were only filling in the gaps. In 1964, Maria Tharp and Bruce Heezen had cobbled together millions of these traces to come up with an underwater chart that showed our planet's system of globe-girdling mid-oceanic ridges in stunning detail. Evidence was mounting that a revolutionary idea, once termed *geopoetry,* was correct. Continents could actually glide across the face of the planet. Aboard ship, continental drift was a forgone conclusion. We saw further evidence of the theory when we landed on St. Peter's and St. Paul's, a jumble of rocks that stick out of the Atlantic Ocean midway between the continents of Africa and South America. They were only fifteen feet tall and covered with tern guano, but that was all right—they are one of the only places on earth where the mid-Atlantic ridge breaks the surface. The other is on the volcano-rich island of Iceland. Darwin collected samples on these same slippery rocks, and oceanographers always make a point of going out of their way to view the famous pilgrimage site.

Albatross and sharks were our constant companions in the South Atlantic. As soon as we stopped to deploy a piece of equipment, the sharks that had been following our wake would catch up and circle about the ship. One night after finishing my midnight plankton tow I wandered back to the stern, where a fifteen-foot-long blue shark was swimming sinuously in and out of the floodlights. She was accompanied by four rainbow runners, exquisitely colored three-foot-long fish who darted back and forth in front of her nose. I watched transfixed for almost an hour. But the rainbow runners were too enticing. They make good eating, and a fishing rod stood nearby. I threw some bait in front of the runners, making sure not to catch the shark by mistake. One by one I landed the elegant fish. Then there was only the blue shark gliding gracefully through the lights.

We kept a chain and shark hook near the stern, and I couldn't help myself. I baited the hook and threw it into the water to lure the shark closer in for a picture. She circled once and came back. I was too late. There was a great shaking of chains. She had taken the bait. I had to call two other shipmates to haul her, thrashing and twisting, aboard. We saved some of the meat for a future fish fry and a crewmember showed me how to remove her jaws. I dried them and took them back to college, but they never gave much pleasure. All I could remember was her grace and beauty that I had sacrificed for such a meaningless souvenir. I was glad when her jaws mysteriously disappeared from my dorm one summer.

By the time we reached Buenos Aires I was homesick for the sight of green vegetation. For the past four months we had seen nothing but turquoise-blue water and puffy white cumulus clouds. I was ready for a change. It turned out that the cruise from Buenos Aires back to Recife would be a nonworking leg. I asked around and was given permission to travel overland by bus. All I had to do was make sure I was back on the dock in Recife nine days later. That didn't seem like a problem. I had taken a bus from Boston to New York. How difficult could this be? What I hadn't counted on was that traveling from Buenos Aires to Recife, Brazil, was more like traveling across the entire United States by bus. Only this trip would take place on dusty unpaved roads in a bus without air conditioning. I had been trying to learn Spanish by listening to tapes in the ship's library and everyone on the bus spoke Spanish, but when we stepped off the bus for meals everyone spoke Portuguese. I still confuse the two languages.

We traveled through some spectacular countryside, from the estancias and pampas of Argentina to the coast and jungles of Brazil. We crossed several rivers several times wider than the Mississippi. The bus would simply emerge from the jungle, trundle down a steep bank and onto a rickety old barge. Twin outboard motors would putter us fitfully across the river, and we would resume our journey up the other side. After several more days we arrived at night in the mountains above Rio de Janeiro. The city shimmered in light below us. Streetlights outlined the famous five beaches that encircle the city. Rio looked like an elegant lady, wearing a stunning string of pearls.

I spent three days sleeping and recovering on the beach. One day a statuesque young woman strode down from the favellas and spread out her blanket. Whispers rippled through the crowd. She was Heloise Pinheiro, the actual girl from Ipenema. The song had been written about her three years before and would be on the top of the charts in the United States on my return. It was with considerable reluctance that I got back on the bus and somehow made it to the right dock, at the right time, in Recife. I was exhausted and had a severe case of dysentery. The *Atlantis II* never looked so good. I crawled into my bunk and slept for the next twenty-four hours.

We had to return quickly from Recife to Woods Hole. We were due to take Vice-President Humphrey on a "show-and-tell" cruise to Maine. Unfortunately, we encountered bad weather and had to cancel a much-anticipated stopover in Barbados. Crew members had been rhapsodizing about the flying fish served at "Dirty Dick's." But I was never to taste their delicate flesh. We had used so much fuel bucking bad weather that we were behind schedule and had to make an emergency landing in Bermuda instead. The bad weather had turned into a hurricane but we still had to refuel.

We threw anchors to windward to try to hold us off the dock, but it didn't work. The ship pounded up against the dock until we finally stove a hole in her side. There was a commotion on deck that night. Two crew members had gone ashore and returned nursing alcoholic grudges against the captain. Officers had to strap guns to their waists and handcuff the crew members to their bunks for the duration of the cruise. It was a tense and unnerving night.

The day before exiting the Gulf Stream, I caught a sea turtle and put it in our onboard aquarium. At the end of my late-night watch I looked in on the turtle and noticed that the water temperature in her tank was dropping. I wound several hot water hoses inside her tank and went to bed satisfied I had solved the problem. The following morning at breakfast, I was greeted with loud guffaws. It seemed the chief engineer had come on duty at midnight to find the ship's water pressure running dangerously low. I had diverted all the ship's hot water through the turtle's water tank! As soon as we landed I rushed the turtle to the National Marine Fisheries' Aquarium in Woods Hole, where she grew quite plump and lived happily for several years.

It had been a spectacular cruise. We had survived the first wreck, the first mutiny, and the first women scientists aboard an oceanographic research vessel—the last, a long overdue and delightful milestone. Plus we had collected data to bolster the new theory of plate tectonics and had helped solve several problems in planktonic and benthic biology. I had been surrounded by a school of a hundred four-foot Barracuda diving off Trinidade Island, and had burst my eardrum while diving to clean the portholes of the bow observation chamber in Dakar. I was more than ready to go back to college!

The Simian Seminars (1967–1970)

A few days before returning to college I called a friend to ask if anything had changed.

"You won't believe it. Everything has changed!"

He was right. When I left in December, Harvard students were expected to wear coats and ties at meals. Women visitors had to be out of the dorms by 10 P.M., and couples were supposed to have at least three feet on the floor at all times—we regarded that rule as more of a challenge than a strict prohibition.

But by September 1967, everything had changed. The campus had blossomed into a heady swirl of long hair, tie-dyes, student protests, free love and grass . . . plenty of grass, and we did inhale, if memory serves.

But I still had a problem. I had decided not to major in biology, but still needed a concentration. My roommate mentioned that a trickle of students had started to switch out of biology into biological anthropology. The molecular wars were starting to take their toll. The "anthro" department might fit me to a "T." It didn't have any chemistry or math requirements, but I could still take all the biology courses I wanted. What I didn't realize was that the switch would put me in the middle of a revolution, which was about to sweep through the fields of anthropology, psychology, and biology.

Irv Devore became my tutor, but not a tutor in the usual sense of the word. Harvard likes to come up with a lot of high-fallutin' terms for mundane things—you had a concentration rather than a major, house rules became parietals or "wall rules," teachers who were assigned to guide you through the ropes of writing an undergraduate thesis were called tutors, not professors.

I could not have been more fortunate. Irv had been one of the first anthropologists to study primates as models to learn about the early evolution of human behavior. He was already starting to attract a wide circle of grad students from many disparate fields. To be included as an undergraduate was a heady experience. It was a badge of high honor to be able to say you were a Devore student. It meant you had access to grants, information, and field research, because Irv was a master fundraiser. He could stay up all night with students, jump onto a plane, prepare a speech, and deliver it the next evening to a group of his Washington peers, who would see that a dozen of Irv's students would receive funding for another year.

Every week, undergraduates, grad students, post docs, and visiting professors would sit on Irv's living room floor to discuss human and primate behavior. The sessions were initially dubbed "boony flicks" because Irv had filmed and studied baboons. They were finally given the formal title "The Simian Seminars," but they evolved into something far greater. Margaret Mead might drop in to discuss Somoa, Louis Leakey early hominids, Dian Fossey gorillas, Roger Payne whales, or E. O. Wilson social ants. If Jane Goodall were flying to the West Coast, she would arrange her flight so she could stop by Irv's house to fill us in on her latest findings. We were among the first to learn of tool use and later infanticide among her chimpanzees in the Gombe Reserve.

The seminar would usually start with Irv introducing a graduate student who had just returned from the field or was working on a particularly tricky theoretical problem. We would settle back with pizza and beer while the speaker used an easel to jot down data, graphs, arguments, and counterarguments.

I remember one session where my section leader, Bob Trivers, was discussing sexual selection. He was arguing that it made Darwinian sense for males to be more sexually active than females. The Harvard students seemed amused, the Radcliffe students annoyed. Several 'Cliffies personally offered to prove Trivers wrong. Other suggested that women were not merely passive bystanders but actively sought out the most promising mates—the subtext being that even rising young graduate students like Trivers were not all that promising as prospective mates.

Frankly, I thought Bob's argument was just a witty justification for his notoriously active sex life. Little did I know he was laying the genetic foundation for a revolutionary new way of looking at animal and human behavior.

After the presentation, everyone would leap into the fray. Sound ideas, outrageous anecdotes, and fallacious absurdities would fly about the room. Irv always led the way. He had a down-home East Texas style that was a relief from the highbrow Cambridge norm. He might draw on his Texas upbringing to describe how hunters used fixed action patterns or biological releasers to fool their prey. In lectures he would refer to certain monkey mating styles as "Slam, bam, thank you Ma'am," something we were unaccustomed to hearing in more traditional Harvard halls. It was said you could hear a pin drop during one of Irv's annual, well-attended lectures on the physiology of the human orgasm. Shock and humor were among the tools of his trade.

Irv was also wise and wonderful. When regular classes were on strike, he gave a moving talk that used his anthropological insight to help put our era in perspective. But it was the little things I remember the most. I still travel with a shaving brush because Irv once mentioned that if you had a decent shaving brush you could always work up a good lather with even the most recalcitrant piece of airline soap.

After midnight the seminars would spread into the kitchen, parlor, and dining room. Knots of animated students would argue, discuss, and cajole. You might hear Irv demonstrate the click language of the Kalahari Bushmen or mimic the mating call of an amorous rhino. The seminars would sometimes continue well into the morning. More than one student learned to dread the sound of the ever-patient Nancy Devore's early-morning footfalls when he realized he had once again abused her hospitality.

One of the discoveries of the seminars was the internalization of what we eventually called "gene thinking." Prior to the sixties, biologists would often state that a particular adaptation evolved for the good of the species or for the good of the group. In the seminars we would routinely jump on anyone, including Irv, who slipped into such sloppy ways of thinking. It became our oft-stated mantra that evolution doesn't work that way. It has to work on the level of genes—and selfish genes at that.

Irv once told us a story that showed the power of gene thinking. He was visiting John Whiting, his colleague in the Social Relations Department, at Whiting's house on Martha's Vineyard. The two spent the day swimming, sunning, and catching blue crabs in the nearby Tisbury pond. That evening the two professors retired to the porch and Irv proceeded to use "gene thinking" to explain why male blue crabs protect female crabs when they molt. It was not for the good of the species. It was not for the good of the female. It was not even for the good of the male. The behavior evolved so the male could be there during the crucial few moments when the female had shed her shell and was able to mate. Only then could he pass on his genes to the next generation. The protection the male seemed to be giving the female when she was most vulnerable was merely the by-product of his genes' selfish behavior.

Whiting sat there looking more and more irritated. Finally he exploded, "Damn your eyes, Devore! I've been looking at blue crabs for thirty years. How can you come down here and figure it all out in fifteen minutes?" He echoed Thomas Henry Huxley's famous lament on hearing Darwin's theory of natural selection, "How, extremely stupid of me not to have thought of that!" Perhaps that's just the way it is— the most original observations always seem the most obvious after someone else has figured them out.

Our new way of thinking was eventually codified and given a name. It became more controversial after E. O. Wilson wrote, *Sociobiology: The New Synthesis.* A scientific revolution was underway. Harvard was the battleground and attending the Simian Seminars was, I suppose, like being part of a terrorist cell. Many of us lived double lives during those days. Leda Cosimedes remembers spending her mornings in the biology department, where she was advised by Bob Trivers, and her nights in the psychology department, where she worked in the pigeon lab started by B. F. Skinner, apocryphally known for raising his daughter in a Skinner box. He was also the father of behaviorism, the school of thought that said that an organism is born as a tabula rasa and that you could use positive and negative reinforcers to teach it how you wanted it to behave. But gene thinking showed that nature puts constraints on human and animal behavior. People didn't want to hear this in the sixties. Consequently, most of us lived double lives. We were politically liberal in a liberal era, but our research kept showing that human nature is not as malleable as we might like to believe. It was often a depressing revelation. The Simian Seminars provided a salon where people interested in the evolution of behavior could speak freely.

Scores of books were the direct result of conversations started at the Simian Seminars. Presentations often initiated a career trajectory or cemented a reputation. Worldviews were molded, graduate students nurtured. Many of these former grad students are now heads of departments in anthropology, psychology, biology, and medicine. Their influence is felt in some of the best universities in the world. Sociobiology, which took a beating in the politically correct eighties, went underground and has reemerged as evolutionary psychology: the branch of psychology that displays the role of genes and evolution in the way we process information and think. Today the ideas of evolutionary psychology affect everything from brain studies to medical care.

There was always a healthy openness to the seminars. Everyone was equal. It was expected that you would say what you really felt. You couldn't hedge. It was the only way the field would progress. You had to say things that sometimes made you feel uncomfortable. It was only by doing so that your ideas could be evaluated, expanded upon or rejected. It was a vital healthy interchange—probably impossible in a politically correct world where standup comedians often utter more insightful truths than academics.

Of course, there were disagreements in our intellectual family. All was not always peaceful. There were hurt feelings, jealousies, sibling rivalries, attacks on authority, and insensitivities to gender issues. At least one student felt slighted and stormed halfway down Massachusetts Avenue before realizing how infantile his or her behavior was.

But the disagreements pushed us to more creative thinking. Some of the most influential feminist anthropologists received their early training by raising the consciousness of some of the Simian Seminars' more retrograde sexists.

Of course, there were some cases of outright sexual discrimination. I remember feeling embarrassed and a little let down that Sarah Hrdy wasn't able to join our all-male team studying rhesus monkeys on an uninhabited island in the Caribbean. She was brilliant, focused, had already written a book, and was generally far better equipped to do field research than any of us males. She went on to produce a landmark study of infanticide among Langur monkeys in India.

We knew we were onto something in the Simian Seminars. We were starting to make sense of seemingly senseless phenomena. But we also knew there were nagging problems—missing links to our theories. We could see that animals and humans made incredibly accurate Darwinian decisions. We could understand why they made them, but we didn't know how they made them. The brain was still regarded as a mysterious black box. It has only been with recent advances in neurobiology that the true import of the Simian Seminars has started to be realized. Brain researchers are unearthing the missing links to the theories we were discussing in our Simian Seminars thirty years before.

One of the observations that evolutionary psychologists have made is that there seems to be a universal human predisposition to create religions. If gene thinking became our religion, then the Simian Seminars were our summer camp. They had that heady evangelical quality to them. Irv, originally the son of a Texas preacher, became our shaman, and we his disciples. If evolutionary thinking has become a new secular religion, it's a pretty good one, more tolerant than many, better at explaining the world than most.

Sitting on Irv's living-room floor in the sixties was like being in London when Darwin was wrestling with the ideas behind natural selection, or in Vienna when Freud was discovering psychoanalysis. It was important to see the process and learn the language. In later years, I would use the insights gained from "gene thinking" in writing about behavior. But it was also important to witness the fascinating but messy process of scientific discovery. A student would come up with a new insight and everyone would take sides and argue about its validity, but agreement would only come years later with the discovery of more data. Evidence was the crucial factor. Unlike theological or political arguments, scientific arguments are eventually resolved and the field goes on to gather new more accurate insights. But the public usually doesn't see this process up close. All they see are the results after all the uncertainty has been resolved. This can make science seem like a very objective, even boring process, but that is not the case. It is an exceedingly active and contentious endeavor.

Today I realize that the insights gleaned from informal meetings like the Simian Seminars have grown inversely as the memory of my formal lectures has declined—or the knowledge of the lectures has become obsolete. I find I often use a chance comment dropped over a beer twenty years before, but seldom use anything from the formal lectures I attended. So I make a point of telling my writing students to pass up interviews with established scientists in favor of joining some grad student in a marsh, at a lab bench, or at a favorite watering hole—attend as many informal science meetings as possible, the "liquidus meetings" of geologists, the "Soc Rel Sherries" of the Social Relations Department, the "herp burps" of herpetologists. It is only when you get a scientist to join you for an "over-a-beer conversation" that you will find out what is really going on in a field, who is really doing good work, and where the field is really heading. You never know when you might pick up one of those pithy, off-the-record quotes that can make your writing sing. The research, you can always get from reading journals. It is a technique political writers have used for years.

Undergraduate Years (1967–1970)

When I took the year off to work on the *Atlantis II*, I figured that at least I would have something to write about. Wrong. I submitted a lyrical essay about studying plankton to a creative writing course and was turned down flat. Attached to my sample was a little note that said, "Your writing is not mature enough for this class."

My rejection was relieved, somewhat, by my acceptance into the Signet Society. The Signet is a singular institution at Harvard. It is made up people who are interested in writing and the arts who meet every day for lunch. While I was concentrating on learning science, the Signet kept me in touch with the writing world.

The dominant characteristic of most Signet members was ambition. I remember hearing long, earnest conversations about whether writers or politicians wielded more power. Coming from a political family, it was an eye-opening conversation. We decided that most Harvard students just wanted to become the next President of the United States but that Signet students wanted to become gods.

Half of the Signet members wrote for the *Harvard Crimson* and are now editors of some the most influential newspapers in the country. As an undergraduate I grew to appreciate the writing and opinions of people like Frank Rich and James Fallows, and today continue to read them in the *New York Times* and the *Atlantic Monthly*. But the other half of our membership seemed to spend all of their time watching television at the Harvard Lampoon. I figured they would never amount to anything. Of course they went on to start the *National Lampoon,* and *Saturday Night Live,* and to write the screenplay for *Animal House,* now considered to be a classic of its genre. I think a road trip I took with the 'Poonies was the basis for a scene in *Animal House,* but I'm not sure. Due to their efforts, today's Lampoon and Signet members have a direct pipeline to the upper echelons of Hollywood's film and comedy worlds.

I still don't know why I was accepted in the Signet. I was quietly studying anthropology at the time. But I do know that part of the reason I write today is to justify my former membership. The Signet has a fine old tradition that says when you are elected to the society you receive a rose that you are supposed to return inside your first published book. I think I gave my rose to someone I was trying to woo, unsuccessfully as I remember it, but I still make a point of giving the first copy of every one of my books to the Signet Society's library.

Harvard wasn't all Simian Seminars and Signet dinners. I took a number of fascinating courses. On the *Atlantis II,* biologists had urged me to take a good geology course, explaining that it was impossible to really understand evolution without a good grounding in geology. Harvard's introductory geology course was Geology 1, informally known as "Rocks for Jocks," but today I find I use it more in my writing than almost any other course. Geology was going through its own revolution in the sixties. In 1915, Alfred Wegner had come up with continental drift, a solid theory with a whimsical name. His prime piece of evidence came from looking at a globe. It was clear that if you moved the African and American continents together they would fit together almost perfectly. He proposed that they had once been attached but had drifted apart as the continents split and the Atlantic Ocean opened. However the drawback of Wegner's theory was that nobody could think of a way that you could move something as massive and heavy as a continent. So his quixotic theory had languished in the dustbin of poetic yet unprovable ideas until the early sixties, when oceanographic vessels like the *Atlantis II* started to map and sample the ocean floor. By 1967, they had come up with a revised version of continental drift called plate tectonics. What plate tectonics lacked in poetry was made up for by its grandeur. Here was a powerful new tool to understand the dynamic history of our planet.

However, Harvard has a long and distinguished career of having at least one prominent faculty member on the wrong side of every major intellectual advance. At a recent graduation, the Dean of Students expressed it best: "We want to congratulate you on your recent graduation from Harvard Medical School. You have learned more than any other preceding class. We must caution you, however, that half of everything you have just learned is wrong. Unfortunately, we just can't tell you which half."

Unlike the biology department, which had tried to hide the molecular wars from the eyes of curious undergraduates, the geology department decided to be more forthright. The faculty was hopelessly divided between "the drifters," who believed in continental drift, and "the transgressors," who thought that all the world's features could be explained by a confusing system of floods and droughts labeled oceanic transgressions and regressions. So, instead of having one professor teach plate tectonics to one section of the class and another professor teaching transgressions to another section, the faculty presented the entire curriculum as a debate. Of course, this led to an uproar. How could you ace an exam if the professor didn't tell you the right answer?

Frankly, I felt the debate was already outdated. Almost all our research on the *Atlantis II* had been geared toward showing that the surface of our planet is covered with massive plates that rest on the earth's viscous mantle. Heat rising from the earth's interior emerges at mid-oceanic ridges and pushes these plates apart. The theory neatly explained why mountains, volcanoes, and deep ocean trenches occur where they do and helped predict where we you could expect to find deposits of gold, silver, oil, and other valuable minerals. Even a rudimentary knowledge of plate tectonics allowed anyone to understand the history and features of his or her own landscape. As a writer, plate tectonics enabled me to describe the fascinating history of our dynamic planet, one of the greatest stories ever told.

I was fortunate to have Stephen Jay Gould as my section leader. I fancied myself as a bit of a hotshot from my time on the *Atlantis II*, so he and I would get into long heated technical arguments in class. We became pretty good friends because of it. More than anything else, Stephen Jay Gould made me aware that a writer could use the theory of plate tectonics to set the scene in writing about the history of life on our planet.

Another memorable course was Plants and Human Affairs. It was taught by Richard Schultes, a kindly old New England professor who had the reserved manner of a nineteenth-century Victorian naturalist and the dry wit of an upcountry family doctor. Dr. Schultes enjoyed telling students about his most hair-raising adventures as if they were no more interesting than a simple walk in the woods. He had short-cropped hair, a clipped New England accent, was deacon of his local church, and had ingested a greater variety of drugs than any other man on earth. His lectures were mesmerizing. He had lived with shamans, collected more than 27,000 medicinal plants, and introduced the psychedelic era with his discovery of psilocybin mushrooms. He would casually note that he could find a fifteen-foot marijuana plants growing within a ten-block area in almost any city. The best place to go was to the Italian sections, where women had always grown marijuana outside their backdoors for use in traditional Italian dishes. They would have been appalled to think they were growing the same drug that hippies were being arrested for smoking. He explained that canaries were no longer popular pets because the only reason they used to sing was that their bird food used to be liberally laced with marijuana seeds. The course drew all the students who thirsted after science, travel, and an occasional legally sanctioned buzz. The high point of the class occurred during our weekly afternoon labs, when we would sample plants flown in from all over the world specifically for our labs. I chewed saliva-inducing betel nut with the future alternative medicine guru Andy Weil, and watched Michael Crichton making a coca-leaf tea as his enormous body straddled three separate chairs.

Whenever I made a trip to a new country I made a point of calling Dr. Schultes first. He had an incredible network of former students scattered around the world. They would invariably be fascinating people who were more than happy to introduce you to the flora and fauna of their countries. I did a lot of traveling in those days. One year I timed my exams so that they all fell on the first few days of exam period. I used the remaining two weeks to deliver a car to Florida, catch a puddle jumper to the Bimini Islands, sleep on the deck of the overnight mail boat to Nassau, and then return to Miami, where I met friends who gave me a ride back to college. I still remember waking up on the mail boat as it slipped into Nassau Harbor beside the incoming banana boats and the outgoing fishing boats. The entire two-week vacation cost me $48. It was the best vacation I ever had. Another time I stayed at the La Paguera marine station in southern Puerto Rico and visited the incredible phosphorescent bay. I still use impressions gained on those trips in my writing today and continue to find isolated biology stations to be incredibly romantic settings full of fascinating people eager to share their knowledge and love of the natural world. I urge potential writers to travel when they are young and have the time. If you don't think you have the money, be creative; that's the best way to meet people and learn about the world.

The peak of my undergraduate experience was doing fieldwork on an uninhabited island off the coast of Puerto Rico. Five of us spent the summers of 1968 and 1969 studying rhesus monkeys as they learned to live off the land on Desecheo Island. The experience would give me firsthand experience in conducting research, and invaluable practice writing for my thesis. That would be my next chapter in the slow process of learning to write naturally.

Desecheo (1969)

It's difficult not to want to wake up on Desecheo Island. The early-morning sun warms your still closed eyes and stirs your naked body. The flaps of our makeshift lean-to open and close in the first breezes of the new tropical day.

I lie on my cot savoring the languid fantasies still rolling through my slowly waking brain. The cries of laughing gulls harmonize with the steady backbeat of incoming surf. But there is work to be done; monkeys to be found.

I get up, stretch, and amble down to one of the many colorful tidepools that dot the shore. We have placed two large trunks of driftwood bamboo over the tidepool so we can watch the incoming surf tumbling over the rocks. Iridescent fish flit beneath my feet and the surf carries my refuse away. It is certainly not an environmentally correct toilet facility, but a glorious way to start the new day.

I join the team of other sleepy researchers beneath the canvas fly that shades our picnic table. Conversation is desultory; our coffee has yet to kick in. We munch on mangoes, limes, and papaya while languidly watching ants crawl across the table. But Dick Henry can't find the foot-long bar of Ivory Soap we use for washing up.

"Where's the soap?"

"Dunno. You put it in the bucket after supper?"

"No, I left it over there on the washing rock. There's only a few shavings left."

"Must have been the land crabs. Swarms of 'em were crawling all over the place last night. I wonder where those buggers hide during the day?"

But the land crabs' cousins, the hermit crabs, are still in evidence. We have marked the shells of each hermit crab with clusters of red nail polish and named them after our favorite professors; "Irv" is the largest, "E. O." the quietest, and "Trivers" the fastest. Our conversation turns finally to the upcoming day. We decide to fan out over the island and keep in touch by walkie-talkie.

I start up the steep path that passes beneath a copse of cool green gumbo-limbo trees. It's a relief to leave the sun and incessant roar of the surf behind. At least the sun is now filtered through beautiful, green, translucent leaves. The path is dappled with patches of darting light, and I can feel beads of sweat already building beneath my shirt.

Desecheo is only 700 feet tall, but its volcanic core rises precipitously out of the sea. Three jungle-covered valleys connected by a steep sharp ridge trisect the island. Rain runs quickly off the ridge, leaving it so dry it only supports wild grasses and prickly pear. Orchards of gumbo-limbo trees dot the gentle slopes, and goats graze among the tangles of impenetrable cactus that thrive on the steep west side of the island.

The monkeys hide in all of these environments and are devilishly difficult to find. After humans, these rhesus monkeys are the most numerous and successful primates on earth. The troop had been airlifted to Puerto Rico to serve as a reserve colony after India banned the exportation of wild animals for research purposes. We are on the island to study the monkeys' social behavior and see how well they have adapted to their new environment. But first I have to find the secretive little things.

I climb to the west ridge and scan the treetops with my binoculars. Sometimes you can see a branch move or hear the occasional scream of a squabbling monkey. But there is nothing. Not even a breath of wind to stir the trees. I check the west slope that plunges down to the cobalt blue waters of the Caribbean. Even from the top of the island I can see the black triangles of triggerfish finning over the white coral sand, eighty feet below the surface. We have never seen the monkeys on this slope and I hope I will never have to descend it. It lies in the rain shadow of the island and is covered with an impenetrable tangle of saguaro and opuntia cactus.

Suddenly there's a movement. But it is only a feral goat, a descendent of one of those released by forward-thinking pirates who wanted a supply of fresh meat in case they had to hide out from Her Majesty's Royal Navy. Modern pirates are still out here as well. Occasionally we see them exchanging contraband in the lee of Desecheo, still a convenient spot, safely out of sight of the *federalistas*.

We had our own run in with federal officials shortly after our arrival. It had not been an auspicious start. We were taking showers in one of the island's infrequent rainstorms when a helicopter swooped over our heads, then landed on the nearby beach. Two men dressed in black suits and ties stepped off the helicopter and introduced themselves as FBI agents. It's difficult to profess your innocence when you are covered with soap and stark naked except for a pair of knee-high rubber boots. It seemed the FBI had been monitoring our walkie-talkie chatter and that the fishermen who had helped ferry our provisions around the island were *Independistas*, well known for wanting to overturn Puerto Rico's status as a commonwealth of the United States.

When the FBI heard that something valuable had been lost when the fishermen's boat had overturned, the agents were sure they had penetrated a gun-running operation. I suppose we did look like the kind of Cheech and Chong revolutionaries who would try to overthrow the island. We explained, with as much dignity as possible, that the only thing we had lost were our marine radio, all of our provisions, and Peter Warshall's Ph.D. thesis, of value only to a small circle of dedicated primatologists. The agents were only mollified after we showed them the pages of Peter's sodden thesis. We wondered what they would think when we started to use our walkie-talkies to call in reports of hip thrusts and stolen copulations.

Having no luck on the ridge, I decided to walk down the draw into the middle valley. As so often happens, as soon as I left the path I stumbled right into the midst of the troop. Most of the monkeys were on the ground snoozing and grooming; others were in the trees foraging lazily for food. Only the infants were active, grappling, wrestling, and tumbling about in piles of dry fallen leaves.

The reason the monkeys were so easygoing was readily apparent. They were extremely efficient omnivores. Even though they had only been on the island for two years, they had learned to exploit all its resources. Older monkeys were busily grabbing great fistfuls of gumbo-limbo berries and stuffing them into their mouths, while younger monkeys were crawling out to the farthest ends of the branches to pluck the youngest, most tender leaves.

On the ground, an older female poked through the spines of an opuntia cactus, trying to extract its juicy red prickly-pear fruit without impaling her fingers. A male drew a stalk of wild grass through his teeth, trying to dislodge its seeds, then stopped to catch and pop a beetle into his mouth.

One of the juvenile monkeys had learned to shake wasp nests out of a tree, hide until the nest quieted down, then rush in to feed on the protein-filled larvae. His playmates had learned to copy his behavior, so it would be passed down as a type of culture to future generations. But the behavior would not pass up the dominance hierarchy, because older monkeys would not pay attention to the antics of younger monkeys.

Within a few square meters, these monkeys were able to find abundant food that required little effort to gather. No wonder they were so relaxed, yet these monkeys have large intelligent brains. What do they use them for?

Part of the answer lies at hand. The monkeys are extremely social, even political animals. When we first arrived on the island, we were thankful to learn just how easy it was to recognize individuals and determine the troop's social structure.

The dominant male was never difficult to find. He was always well groomed, held his head high, and moved through the troop with ease and assurance. Less dominant monkeys would move aside at his approach and assume a submissive posture. He was usually surrounded by several high-ranking females, their infants, and older offspring. After only a few days, we were able to determine most of the rest of the dominance behavior by carefully noting which monkey gave way when two monkeys met.

One day I received a memorable lesson in how quickly they learn their place in the dominance hierarchy. Normally the monkeys would ignore me as I sat on a rock or stood to the side quietly scribbling notes. But on this day, I happened to step back and accidentally crunch the tail of a female we called "black ear." She shrieked, and from that day on all the monkeys below "black ear" in the dominance hierarchy would give way when I approached and all the monkeys above "black ear" would adopt dominant postures. They recognized me as fitting in just above "black ear," but below "double notch." I have been put in my place many times since, but never with such precision.

After a few more hours, the troop moved on. It was not a coordinated move. The dominant male simply stood, yawned, and sauntered down the valley. The other animals followed. The females scooped up their infants and placed them quickly on their bellies, where the little ones would hang upside down, clinging to their mothers' long abdominal fur with their tiny hands and feet.

The whole group wandered down the valley to a tall old gumbo-limbo tree. It didn't look any different from the other gumbo-limbo trees, but the male knew this tree had a deep cleft in its trunk where rainwater collected. He thrust his hand into the hole, raised it, and slurped the water as it cascaded down the crease in the heel of his palm.

After a few more handfuls, he moved off and the next most dominant monkey drank her fill. The monkeys continued down the dominance hierarchy, but with each successive monkey the amount of water decreased. By the time the fortieth monkey dipped her hand into the hole it came out barely moist. Frustration was evident among the thirty thirsty monkeys at the bottom of the hierarchy.

The group moved on but tension was rising. "NV" tried to mount one of the dominant male's cousins. She cuffed his face and the dominant male had to intervene. Fights broke out instantly between several other monkeys. After the conflicts subsided, one of the males walked purposefully down the draw. Three females with infants followed. They would establish a separate troop. Over the course of several weeks another subdominant male accompanied by females would also split off and establish a separate colony with its own territory and water holes.

"NV" had been bitten badly on the hand. He fled down the valley, shrieking and alone. He went into isolation and deteriorated quickly. The next day we saw him he was emaciated and unkempt from lack of grooming. He already seemed defeated. A few days later, wild screams brought us to the shore. We found "NV" alone on a rock, his back to the surf, trying to fight off a dozen females. He was now an outcast with no allies, and they seemed to know it. "NV" suffered several more wounds, and a few days later we found the remains of his mangled corpse. Monkeys, like humans, are highly social animals. Without their society, neither they, nor we, are truly primate—or human.

We could see that the ultimate reason the group had split apart was because its environment had changed. As the dry season had progressed, the entire group had become too large for the limited amount of water in the tree-trunk holes. It made sense for the group to split apart and for each troop to establish a territory with its own supply of water.

But the monkeys had not gone through such an analytical cost-benefit analysis. The three dominant males simply reacted to the rising tensions by fighting among themselves. But the fighting had not been random. They had fought only those monkeys that would enhance or decrease their status. They knew exactly who to attack, because the fights were simply skirmishes in a long-standing power struggle. They knew who to back up and who would back up them, because they had made family-based alliances ahead of time.

The monkeys had evolved to behave according to drives for power and status, mediated by neurotransmitters. But the outcome of that behavior often represented the best environmental decision as well. The monkeys in the troop didn't realize the fights and schisms were being caused by environmental changes; they regarded them solely as fights between males. But how often do humans recognize the proximate and ultimate causes for their own behavior? Are elections decided more on issues or status and personality?

Back on Desecheo, the troop was moving purposefully again. This time the monkeys were scampering above us in the canopy. Something was afoot. Suddenly, white-footed brown boobies started to squawk, scream, and fly from their large unkempt nests. With mounting horror I realized what was happening. The monkeys were raiding the boobies' nests. They raced through the trees, snatching eggs, biting off their tops and drinking their contents. In less than half an hour over 300 eggs and chicks had been bitten, eaten, or hurled out of their nests. I knew the monkeys would have to be taken off the island, and our research terminated.

The monkeys' brains had evolved enough to discover how to exploit one of the island's most valuable resources, but not enough to know when to stop. They had not been selected to live on an island with finite resources.

With a heavy heart, I trudged back up the mountain to the easternmost ridge. I found the monkeys sitting on the rocks, quietly digesting their food and recovering from the day's excitement.

As the sun set, wave upon wave of red-footed boobies started to return to their nesting colonies. Suddenly a large, black-winged frigate bird swooped out of a rose-colored cloud toward the scattering birds. The boobies wheeled, rolled, and sideslipped, trying to shake off their agile pursuer. But finally the frigate bird drove a single booby just above the water. The booby had no room to maneuver; it gave up and regurgitated. That was all the frigate had been after; he swooped in and caught the offal before it had time to reach the water. It had been a spectacular aerial duel against a fittingly Wagnerian sunset.

Now the streetlights were starting to switch on along the faraway shores of Puerto Rico. Strings of lights snaked up through the distant valleys. A yellowish glow appeared behind the mountains before a huge full moon rose with transcendent majesty. It loomed over the landscape, dwarfing mountains, homes, and valleys. It rose more rapidly and seemed unnaturally larger than in the Temperate Zone. It looked like it might be more at home rising over an alien planet. I felt strangely in touch with my own ambiguous primate heritage.

The monkeys seemed to be equally mesmerized by the scene. They groomed in silence, occasionally murmuring quietly among themselves. It was as if they were quietly telling jokes in an atmosphere of contentment, harmony, and good will. I could see their fascination with the rapidly rising moon. Had the monkeys assembled on the ridge to watch the moonrise? Had they known it was going to be a full moon? It would have not surprised me. It took little imagination to believe our ancestors could have learned the beginnings of language, science, art, time, and religion while watching similar moonrises millions of years before.

Chapter 3

Getting Started

🐛

At Sea and Wet Behind the Ears:
Writing and Graduate School (1970–1971)

O f course, I couldn't write my thesis the way I just wrote the previous chapter. That would entail using the passive voice of objective scientific discourse, "the beaker was removed and the supernatant decanted," or in our case, "the troop was observed sitting on the East Ridge"; no pique, no humor, no mention of strange moonrises, and certainly no speculating about the origins of language, calendar time, or religion!

However, I knew that we had been given a unique opportunity, and that I wanted to write about it. Since our work had been funded by the National Science Foundation, you could also say that taxpayers had a right to read about our research—even if they didn't want to. I would even argue that we should not consider the scientific process to be really complete until its results have appeared in the mainstream press. We owe that much to the public who pays for most of our modern research.

I could have written about our monkeys as a reflection of mankind's early social development, or our discovery that the introduced monkeys had destroyed one of the last breeding colonies of brown boobies in the Caribbean, or about our social research, which was so similar to the work of Jane Goodale. All these angles would have made interesting stories, but there were really only two basic outlets for such writing: *Scientific American* for professional scientists, and *National Geographic* for laymen. I didn't have the credentials to write for *Scientific American* nor good enough photos to submit to *National*

Harvard University Bulletin photo, 1970.

Geographic. Few of today's large-circulation nature and scientific magazines were in existence then, and major newspapers had yet to establish their weekly science sections. But mostly I didn't have the time to pursue these avenues, and, of course, competition was severe.

Perhaps the most difficult thing for a young writer to figure out is when to make the plunge into full-time writing, and how to arrange your life to make that possible. Nineteen seventy was not the right time. I could get drafted! Of course, a few future writers did get drafted and were able to start their careers from that experience. Like many in my generation, I opposed the war but still wonder if I didn't miss out on something by not serving. Vietnam was the defining moment for my generation, and it was important that people were writing about both the war and our opposition to it.

I did put together a proposal for a book based on the experiences of a young monkey we had observed on Desecheo. He had broken away from the main troop, joining up with another, then reunited both troops during the wet season. It smacked of the two great bugaboos of scientific writing, popularism and anthropomorphism. My advisor warned me against writing anything that might taint my scientific career. But I already had the feeling that I wanted to taint my scientific career. I had learned that science exposed you to experiences that people might want to read about, but that only you, your advisor, and perhaps your mother would ever want to read your thesis.

Alas, the thesis had to be written. I finally buckled down and used our data to write a thesis on how an individual relates to the larger group in *Macacca mulatta* society. Of course, it turned out that writing a thesis was a valuable experience. I not only learned that I could actually sit down and write one, but I also learned that there are good, solid reasons why a research paper should be written as objectively and dispassionately as possible. I'm not one of those gung-ho popular science writer types who preach that scientists should start writing like novelists. Brighten it up a bit, sure, but remember there is a difference between writing science and writing about science. In the first instance you are trying to convey research in the most objective way possible; in the second instance, you are trying to illuminate the human side of science.

I'm reminded of a course I taught at Woods Hole. Several of my students were recently retired scientists who wanted to write about their often-illustrious careers. They would regale our class with long, wonderful, warm, and insightful stories about their lives, but they couldn't put those same stories down on paper. Throughout their entire careers they had been taught to write objectively and had picked up the idea that scientific writing was somehow superior to Standard English. I had to explain to them that for all those years they had been taught the wrong way to write, and that now it was okay to start writing naturally. I told them it was all right to write the way they actually felt and thought. It was okay to write about what went wrong and what went right in their research, and what it felt like to make a major breakthrough. It was even all right to make a speculation or two, and to admit to occasional feelings of triumph or jealousy.

They looked at me incredulously. Didn't I know about subjective writing and peer review panels? It usually took them several tries, but once they started to write naturally the logjam was broken and we couldn't get the scientists to shut up. I may be asked to turn in my national Science Writers card for saying this, but I still think scientists write better books about science than professional science writers. They just have to get over their bad writing habits before they start. This used to be less of a problem when scientists had to support themselves through their writing and popular lectures. Publishers had to relearn these lessons as well. Editors at the Harvard University Press still rue the day they turned down *The Double Helix,* James Watson's tell-all book about his quest for the Nobel Prize—perhaps the best book ever written about the culture and inner workings of cutting-edge science.

But writing a thesis was one thing, and figuring out what I wanted to do with my life was quite another. I knew I had been incredibly fortunate to have watched the revolutionary changes sweeping through the sciences. I had been close enough to hear the grinding of gears as several fields had shifted mightily into new paradigms. I knew how fascinating these discoveries were and realized that people were eager to hear about them. I had a burning desire to make films and write about these changes; what I didn't know was where or how to start. About the only career model open to anyone interested in writing about science was to do research and teach in college, while writing and perhaps filming on the side. But even that model was shaky. People like Stephen Jay Gould and E. O. Wilson had not yet started writing, and people like Lewis Thomas and Konrad Lorenz had only written popular books well after their scientific careers had been established. Sarah Blaffer Hrdy, who had not been allowed to join us on Desecheo because of her gender, would follow that model to a "T": teaching, doing research, and writing *Langurs of Abu, The Woman Who Never Evolved,* and *Mother Nature.* Interestingly enough, it was often woman scientists like Jane Goodall who started to create a new paradigm by concentrating more on their research and writing than climbing the academic ladder, so slippery with the moldy accretions of dead wood and sexism.

All these things were in the process of changing. Astronauts walked on the moon the first summer we were on Desecheo, and the first Earth Day was held in 1970. I remember the moon landing vividly because I had just been airlifted to San Juan after bursting my eardrum diving on Desecheo. I had joined friends watching the landing, but it had seemed strangely unreal on television. Afterward we decided to see the film *2001,* enhancing the experience by sitting in the front row of the theater imbibing brownies laced with hash. For two hours we ducked and weaved as space vehicles whooshed by our seats. On the way home we turned on the car radio just as Buzz Aldrin was having trouble redocking his landing craft to the orbiter. We were on the edge of our seats as the two vehicles crept closer and closer and finally clicked into place. The movie had made the real feat unforgettably moving.

The moon landing had helped the television networks consolidate their power at the top of the media food chain. Walter Cronkite was the kindly old professor who led us through the science and excitement of space exploration, while Jacques Cousteau was the dashing young conquistador who inspired us with his sense of adventure and sexy French accent. Newspapers were desperately trying to pull features writers out of Washington bureaus and off statehouse beats to cover these fascinating new topics. They had yet to realize that what they really needed were young writers already trained in the sciences.

It is safe to say I was a pretty confused young man in those days. I had thoroughly enjoyed my undergraduate years and would have been more than happy to continue them in graduate school, but I also felt there were just too many other interesting things going on in the world to be stuck in school for six more years while restricted to a single discipline. But I did realize that graduate school could give you access to fascinating things to film and write about, so I applied to Harvard's anthropology department, for their sole slot in biological anthropology. But I also had a backup plan.

When I had worked on the *Atlantis II,* a biologist had told me that all the interesting science had already been done in the oceans, and that the really important field was going to be Law of the Sea: a new branch of international law that was going to devise new legal regimes to govern fisheries, pollution, and deep sea mineral mining. Unfortunately, I believed him, so I had also applied to the Fletcher School of International Law and Diplomacy. I suppose I had images of getting paid to fly around the world attending important conferences and solving the world's problems. But mostly, when I get confused and have to make a major life decision, I have this unfortunate habit of opting for the more establishment path, even when it doesn't feel right. Besides, I could get an M.A. in international law in one year, instead of a taking six years to earn a Ph.D. It seemed like a good backup, but actually it was a cop-out. My experience at Fletcher was mostly a bust. I knew from day one that I had made a terrible mistake, but I also knew that I could do anything for a year—my thesis had taught me that!

It was during this time that Soviet trawlers were plying our nation's coasts pulse fishing for species like cod, haddock, and hake. The New England fishing industry was up in arms, and newspapers and television stations were scrambling to cover the crisis. But none of the stories showed the Soviet trawlers up close. They were just big menacing presences, manned by equally menacing Soviet functionaries. I decided to write a paper about the joint U.S.–Soviet Fisheries research program operating out of Woods Hole, but I also realized it would make a fascinating news story. On a whim, I wrote to the head of the U.S. Fisheries Lab in Woods Hole asking if it might be possible to go out on one of the Soviet fishing vessels. I thought it would take months of red tape to get permission and that I would finally be turned down flat. Instead, he called right back and asked if I could be ready in a week. If I didn't blow it, this could be the chance of a lifetime. I raced around like a crazy man: getting permission to cut classes, borrowing a movie camera from a friend, and talking Boston's Channel Five television station into lending me some film. I had cut my teeth filming peace demonstrations in Washington for an undergraduate film class. Besides working beside Tommy Werner (who would soon become famous for producing *The Cosby Show* and buying the Red Sox), I had learned in the class valuable lessons in how to improvise in the field. You could always snip a twig off a tree to replace the backup spool you forgot to pack back in the studio!

The cruise only lasted for two weeks but it seemed like I was away for years. Working on a Soviet trawler was not like staying in a hotel in Moscow. It was much more like being sentenced to hard labor in the Gulag Archipelago. The only toilet facility was a small hole cut into the deck, which you had to position yourself over by holding onto an upright pole. The food, which I had been looking forward to as exotic, turned out to be an endless supply of watery cabbage soups and black bread that looked wonderful but tasted like corrugated cardboard. Every morning we woke to the sounds of the *Internationale* played over the intercom, followed by announcements for the day's meetings of various Communist cells. Everyone knew who the ship's Party informants were, and conversations would veer swiftly off course in their presence. I was startled one day when I happened to turn on the radio and could just hear the Harvard Dartmouth football game. It felt like we were on the other side of the world, but we were really only twelve miles off the U.S. coast.

Our days consisted of weighing and counting fish. It was not rocket science. The way you sex a flounder is to hold it up to the light. If you could see through it, it was a male—if not, a female. The nets would come in bulging with a bouillabaisse of species. Heads, tails, and distended abdomens would stick through the mesh like creatures you would see in a painting by Hieronymous Bosch. A crewman would untie the codend of the net and a silvery cascade of fish would spill into the collecting table and overflow onto the deck. We would wade in to count, weigh, and measure the slippery creatures. Sometimes you could slip a prize fish to the cook for a break from his endless supply of borscht. I started to pick up a few words of Russian and could

Aboard the Soviet fisheries vessel the R/V *Blesk*. *Courtesy of the* Boston Globe.

do a fair impression of Leo Tolstoy when counting off our "doh cent centimetras." One day, one of the Soviet scientists reached into the net and almost fell over backward. A six-foot-long torpedo fish lurking beneath the pile had shocked him. Fortunately, the torpedo fish had already discharged most of its biological battery coming to the surface in the crowded net.

The amount of fishing activity was impressive. At night, the lights of East German, Polish, Soviet, Canadian, and Spanish vessels looked like cities at sea. In their small boats, U.S. fishermen could only come out this far for a few days or weeks at a time, but these large subsidized fleets regularly stayed at sea for six months to a year.

The Soviets did it strictly for the money. They could make twice as many rubles at sea as in an equivalent job on shore. I became friends with Vasily, the third mate of our ship. He had gone to sea to support his brother, one of the dissonant sculptors in Moscow. Vasily hated the Soviet system and loved American Beat poets. He wanted to become a translator and confided that the best way to get ahead in Moscow was to have an affair with the wife of one the Party's top officials, evidently something he had a fair amount of experience with. I also liked our taciturn captain, who had formerly been the captain of a Soviet nuclear submarine. He laughed when he boasted that he knew every centimeter of our Eastern Seaboard. I believed him. Nobody liked the informers.

Toward the end of our cruise we visited the fleet's mother ship. This was a large, impressive factory ship. We saw the huge freezers, where the catch would be frozen for delivery to Kaliningrad six months later. We saw the nets bulging with fish, and we went up on the upper deck where the fishermen played volleyball, flirted with the many female crew members, and lay in the meager sun. During all these times I was discreetly shooting footage. The captain of the mother ship hadn't been sure what do when I had jumped off the tender with my camera in hand. But by that time I had made friends among the Soviet crew who had assured him I was all right.

When we arrived back in Woods Hole, the U.S. Fisheries Service threw a party for the crew of all the ships participating in the survey. It was amusing to see the nationality types emerge as the party progressed. The Russians started the evening standing about awkwardly in their ill-fitting black suits. But by the end of the night, they were giving great bear hugs to their "good American friends." I was sure that Vasily, who had developed a crush on one of our female American scientists, was going to get drunk and defect on the spot. He explained that Russians were just big, blond, romantic Italians at heart.

The following morning we were all still a little bit hung over, an expression that sent Vasily into peals of laughter. The *Boston Herald* was there to take pictures. But just as the cameraman was about to take his

Just before the photographer took this picture, one of the Soviet crewmen gave the author a great big vodka-induced hug. The next day we appeared, head to shaggy head, on the cover of the *Boston Herald.* The photo elicited a deluge of derogatory letters about coddling Soviet fishermen. *Courtesy of the* Boston Herald.

shot, one of the crewmen, a great big bear of a Russian, reached out and gave me a great big, vodka-induced hug. The next day, there we were, wreathed in slightly inebriated smiles, head to shaggy head on the cover of the *Boston Herald.* The photos elicited a deluge of letters critical of me and my father for coddling communist fishermen!

Just before I stepped off the boat, Vasily pulled me aside and passed me a rolled up copy of their Soviet chart of Cape Cod. I tucked it into my jacket and debarked with as nonchalant an air as I could muster. Today the chart hangs in our house on Cape Cod. You can see that it had been lifted off a copy of a 1946 U.S. Coast Guard chart. Our house is about a quarter of an inch off on both charts, and the Kennedy compound is marked in red!

That afternoon I drove straight to Channel Five, where we developed and edited the film. The story was featured on that night's news, and the following morning I received a call from the precursor to *Sixty Minutes:* Would I be willing to sell the film? After thinking for the merest flick of a millisecond, I agreed. Was journalism always going to be so simple? Senator Kennedy's staff members called a few months later, asking if they could show the film to Congress, where they were debating the 200-mile fisheries limit. My only mistake was in not securing rights to the film! It was trotted out for years, whenever the station was doing a story on the plight of the New England fisheries industry. But I had caught the journalism bug, and knew I had a pretty good nose for stories, but was still wet behind the ears and needed a job!

Cape Cod or Caracas? Think Global, Write Local! (1970–1980)

After finishing the Fletcher School, I won a grant for a United Nations graduate studies program on international environmental issues that was based in Geneva. The program would also allow me to attend the preparatory sessions for the Law of the Sea conference, which were taking place in Geneva at the same time. My ultimate goal was to land a job preparing for the Law of the Sea conference that was scheduled to take place in Caracas in 1974. The purpose of the United Nations conference was to establish legal regimes to manage the world's fisheries, offshore oil, and seabed minerals. Until this time there had been virtually no international laws to govern the oceans, which made up three quarters of our planet's surface.

The preparatory meetings were scheduled to take place in New York, London, Geneva, and Malta. It was a beguiling prospect for someone who liked to travel and kibitz with other people concerned about the fate of the world's resources.

But the wheels of the United Nations bureaucracy turn slowly, and I returned to Boston still needing a job. On the flight home I spotted an ad for a new organization called the Science Education Association. SEA was looking for a naturalist for its tall ship cruising to the Galapagos Islands. I applied immediately, but something strange kept happening during the interviews. The directors kept calling me back to ask how organized I was, and whether I had ever raised any money. I was just out of college, for God's sake, what did I know about raising money? I probably should have smelled a rat. But finally the directors asked if I wanted to become the assistant director of the organization, which planned to put college students on a tall ship to study oceanography. My year on the *Atlantis II* had changed my life forever. It was enticing to think I could help start an organization that would offer that experience to other students. But I never thought it through. Instead of diving among the reefs of the Galapagos, I found myself sitting in a cold office in Boston working long hours so that other people could do what I wanted to do. Instead of becoming another Charles Darwin, I was becoming another Bob Cratchitt. I had forgotten my mentor Ken Read's oft-quoted maxim, "At all costs, avoid administration!"

I carried Ken's wisdom to my next job at Earthwatch Expeditions. Earthwatch was another one of the many innovative educational programs established in the seventies. It was based on the idea that people would be willing to pay for the experience of working on a scientific expedition. It would be an equal trade. The participants would gain a rewarding experience, and the scientists would gain a team of willing assistants and much needed funds. I started out in the office writing brochures and licking envelopes, but soon I realized I had the opportunity to write a proposal to start a marine ecology project on Cape Cod. I would be back on Pleasant Bay, studying worms, crabs, and bugs. The grant came through for the summer of 1973.

The program started off on the wrong foot. Right after our students flew in from Texas, Hawaii, and New York, the building inspector drove up to inform us that according to a town ordinance nobody could sleep in the tents. We had to take down the tents and squeeze the students back into the spare rooms and attic of my long-suffering parents' house.

Things improved. During that first summer, we discovered that collectors from the Marine Biological Laboratory in Woods Hole were catching horseshoe crabs in Pleasant Bay, then returning them a few days later. This was curious. We made some inquiries and discovered that they were bleeding the crabs and that the crabs' processed blood was worth over $15,000 a quart. An extract of the blood was being used experimentally to diagnose spinal meningitis and test for Gram-negative bacteria that cause septic shock and such often-fatal diseases as tuberculosis, plague, gonorrhea, and the rabbit-borne disease tularemia.

The following summer we arranged for a joint program with the

MBL. It agreed to pay us a dollar a crab, and we agreed to build large pens so we could hold the crabs and monitor their recovery after being bled in Falmouth. Our long-term goal was to see if you could establish a system of ocean ranching to support this valuable new biomedical industry. This was also an ideal situation for a small startup lab. We had an important research area to investigate and grants to supply us with students. Most importantly, because the MBL wanted 250 crabs twice a week, we also had a self-sustaining, independent source of income to keep us afloat. It was also obvious that the test was going to be commercialized, and it would make perfect sense to have a small, independent field station specifically set up to study this animal that was about to become indispensable to modern medicine.

Besides, I have always had a romantic view of small, isolated biological field stations. On the *Atlantis II* we visited the Bermuda Biological Research Station; in Puerto Rico I stayed at the La Paguera lab; and in South America I had dredged the Recife River with a French scientist working at a remote lab in Brazil. He spent his days diving in the clear waters off Brazil and his nights writing papers on tropical reefs. I loved working in the field with such a dedicated scientist, and wanted to be able to recreate that experience and share it with our students.

Unfortunately, I couldn't be on the Cape for our second year. I was hired by the Sierra Club to present a series of seminars at the Law of the Sea conference being held in Caracas in 1974. I had run into another reality as well. I couldn't afford to just work in the lab during the summers. I had to have a full-time job, and all my jobs required me to work year-round. I lacked the credentials for an academic job that would give me the summer off to run a lab, but fortunately George Buckley did have those credentials. George was a born teacher and became the chief scientist of the lab, which would become one of Earthwatch Expedition's longest running and most successful projects.

My time in Caracas was well spent. I showed the film I had taken aboard the Soviet trawler to the assembled delegates. The head of the Soviet Ministry of Fisheries came up afterwards and slapped me rather too heartily on the back, bellowing, "Good job! Good job!" "My ship! My ship!" Later he would be executed for bribery in the former Soviet Union's notoriously corrupt Caspian Sea caviar industry.

Caracas was transfixed with the oceans throughout the summer of the 1974 conference. Much of the fascination came from a special television series that was being shown on Venezuelan television throughout the conference. *La Planeta de Agua* was hosted and produced by René Ottolini, a remarkable man who could interview his guests in either Spanish, French, English, Portuguese, or his own native Italian, then translate the interview back to Spanish for his Venezuelan audience. His programs were both intelligent and entertaining. They drew an 80 percent viewership in Venezuela, an astounding number much higher than reigning television personalities in the United States like Johnny Carson and Walter Cronkite.

René invited me to appear on his program and show several of my films. After our interview, he asked if I would like to do some underwater filming for his show. Underwater filming is tricky. I had only done a little of it with Ken Read, but had brought along my underwater light meter just in case. I figured, "So what's the worst that can happen? The film will come back blank and I will be found out and fired. But at least I will have had a nice weekend diving." To my utter astonishment the film came back correctly exposed, and every weekend thereafter the Ottolinis would fly me to different coastal locations to film.

René was a remarkably talented, entertaining, and liberal-minded person. He was easily the most popular and therefore one of the most powerful people in Venezuela. He owned and flew his own plane and later ran for the presidency of Venezuela. He would have won the elections hands down except that he was killed in a suspicious accident while flying his plane to a campaign stop on the Caribbean Island of Los Roques—an accident that changed the history of Venezuela in ways we are still witnessing today.

I also befriended Thor Heyerdahl. I had invited him to give a presentation on ocean pollution to the Law of the Sea delegates. He had seen balls of oil floating in the middle of the Pacific Ocean while crossing it on his famous *Kon Tiki* and *Ra* raft expeditions. I noticed how much more attention people paid to a scientist who had actually witnessed these things than to a lawyer droning on about threats to the environment.

After Thor's seminar I happened to mention that I had seen some interesting sculptures of crocodilelike creatures in a newly excavated ruin in Colombia. Our guide had insisted that they were just large sculptures of lizards, but they had teeth and were much larger than a South American caiman. What were they doing in the mountains of Colombia? Heyerdahl was instantly fascinated. He felt they might be depiction's of actual crocodiles made by Egyptians who he believed might have traveled to South America by boat.

After the conference ended, we flew to Bogotà and traveled deep into the jungles of Colombia to visit the ruins. When we returned to the city several days later, it was 3:00 A.M. and all the hotels were full. No problem. Heyerdahl had experience getting out of such jams. He conferred with the driver, who took us to a brothel in one of the fanciest suburbs of Bogotà. Management gave us extra rooms and we spent the night sleeping in the lap of luxury. The next morning I had to catch a 6 A.M. flight back to Caracas. Since it was so early, I didn't bother to shave or change out of the clothes I had been riding in for several days. Big mistake. As I was waiting for the plane, two soldiers grabbed me from behind and dragged me to a small building in back of the airport. They were only about sixteen years old, but they toted large, lethal-looking submachine guns. They started to snap a few pictures with my camera, but when they started to open its back to remove my film I reacted. It contained all the photos that I hoped to use in an article about traveling through Colombia with Thor Heyerdahl. My passport had an official stamp from the Law of the Sea conference. I slammed the passport down on the table and bellowed with as much affronted dignity as I could muster, "*Yo soy diplomatico!*" They exchanged nervous glances and let me go. I hate to think what they might have done to the man behind me without such an improbable excuse. I missed my plane and headed back to the brothel, where Thor Heyerdahl was enjoying a lucious tropical breakfast surrounded by an adoring circle of some of the most beautiful women I have ever seen. He was entertaining them with the same stories he had been telling to the delegates of the Law of the Sea conference!

These were pretty heady experiences for a young man from New England. But by the end of the summer, I had had enough of such adventures. I had the feeling that you could spend your entire career working on Law of the Sea issues and never see any results. I realized that I preferred to accomplish something concrete on a local level, rather than fritter away my time on international negotiations that might never come to fruition.

But mostly I missed our little lab on Cape Cod. I had started it with my girlfriend and two friends. We felt the lab was important and could make a significant impact on both our students and the local community. I was also ready to get married. Was I in for a big surprise! I had been in constant touch with my girlfriend, who had stayed on the Cape to run the lab. I don't know what I had been thinking, but by the time I returned, she had fallen in love with my former business partner.

This was the beginning of an intensely bittersweet interlude. I had returned to the Cape thinking I had finally found my life's work. But instead I discovered I had lost someone whom I had hoped would be my life's companion. We had spent months before I went to Caracas planning how we would run the lab on my return. We had partnered up with Skip Norgeot, the town's former shellfish warden. Skip had grown up swimming, fishing, and hunting on Pleasant Bay and had collected the stories of the old-timers who had scratched out a living from its richly productive waters. He was also a practical man with a poetic streak who wanted to introduce kids to his way of life. He had a family, a job, and knew exactly who he was and where he belonged. I envied him for his stability and self-knowledge. I felt like I had been vainly flailing about trying to figure out the same things, which seemed to be his by birthright.

In my naiveté, I forgot that Skip was also devilishly handsome and that both he and my girlfriend had been recently divorced. When I returned from my adventures in South America I discovered that Cindy had fallen deeply in love with Skip. I felt like I had lost both my life's companion and the ability to carry on my life's work. I plunged back into running the lab and working with our students. But soon the days grew shorter and the students drifted back down our long dusty driveway to their own lives and worlds.

It was also the first week of September, traditionally the time when my seasonal affective disorder switches from the hypomania of summer to the first deep depressions of autumn. I felt totally alone and abandoned. But slowly I started to function. I continued to collect crabs until they too migrated offshore for winter. I started to teach some adult education classes in marine biology, but mostly I began to write. Malcomb Hobbs, the much-revered editor of our local paper, offered me a job chronicling the life of Pleasant Bay for a series of weekly features in *The Cape Codder*. I tried to combine our observations about the marine biology of the bay with some of the new insights coming out of animal behavior studies. But mostly, I tried to convey my love for the bay with all its poignant yet subtle beauty. I believe my writing was improved by the intensity of the feelings I was experiencing at the time. Although this was a lonely and painful period in my life, it was also extremely rewarding and would become a model for future years.

I developed a natural routine. I got up every morning at sunrise and spent several hours writing before going out in my boat to collect specimens or do research in the lab. I discovered this was my natural rhythm for writing as well. This was a revelation. Before, I had followed the customary student's pattern of procrastinating for weeks, before finally writing my papers all in one swoop the night before they were due. I soon discovered that I needed the harsh light of early morning to sharpen and improve my style. I know other writers say they do all their writing at night, but I'm suspicious. I find that anything I write at night inevitably has to be rewritten the next day. All the writing I thought had been so clever the night before is revealed to be nothing but clichés and sloppiness under the harsh light of morning. I often make the analogy that writing is like playing chess: You can only stayed focused for a few hours at a time, and after that, everything you write turns to mush. Today I write for two to three hours every morning and do research or make calls in the afternoon. I usually try to do this six days a week, or even seven if I am on a tight deadline.

Mostly I discovered how much I liked the process of writing. It became an almost Zen-like experience: diving, collecting insights, translating them into concise little essays. I grew attuned to the light and nature around me. I regained my childhood ability to see things in the water that other people couldn't see. The experience was more intense because I was alone. In many ways it was a wonderful three months. But I knew it couldn't last. Winter was fast approaching, I needed another job, and it was clear I had truly lost my girlfriend. My essays in *The Cape Codder* had been well received, but I couldn't afford to live on what I was being paid. Still, that was not the point. I had tasted the writer's life and knew that somehow I had to make it my own.

The time was not yet right. After a few months, I received a call from Peter Chermayeff, who had been hired to design the National Aquarium in Baltimore. They were looking for a director. It was a fascinating project. Peter was charged with designing a world-class aquarium, using water, light, and sound to create the impression that visitors were truly beneath the sea. I was hired as director and worked with Peter Chermayeff, who had already designed the New England aquarium and would go on to become the world's foremost designer of large-scale aquaria. He had a showman's knack for designing fascinating displays. After a consultant suggested using models to depict continental drift, I remember Peter saying that live animals always make the best exhibits.

The New England Aquarium was best known for its giant reef tank. Visitors were invited to walk up a broad ramp that spiraled around the cylindrical tank looking in on the fish at all levels of a simulated coral reef. One weekend I went home and thought, "Wouldn't it be wonderful if, instead of having a cylindrical tank where people stand on the outside looking in, we could make a donut-shaped tank where visitors would be on the inside looking out at giant fish and water! And couldn't we perhaps build a giant greenhouse on top of the aquarium so people could walk down through a living rainforest to enter the aquarium?" I sketched out my ideas using my best third-grade sketching skills and handed the results to Peter the following morning. Chermayeff glanced at my childlike drawings and dismissed them with an airy wave of his hand, "That would never work. The concrete couldn't stand up to all that extra weight and the panes would crack." A few weeks later the blueprints came back. There was my greenhouse and donut-shaped tank done in the most professional of renderings!

But again, as summer approached, my seasonal affective disorder-induced hypomania kicked in, and I desperately wanted to be back at our own little lab. This time I had learned my lesson. It had taken a decade, but I finally realized I would never be able to accomplish what I wanted until I went out on my own. As soon as I made this decision, things started to fall into place. I got married and had my son Ben, a

Filming the Iktoc oil spill aboard a helicopter in Mexico.

talented artist who is presently making his own decisions about choosing stability or the artistic life. I also received contracts to produce a slide tape about Georges Bank, was hired as a consultant to create an maritime school in East Harlem, and wrote freelance articles for *Smithsonian* magazine, the *Boston Globe,* and *Harvard Magazine.*

In 1979 I was hired to film the effects of the Iktoc oil spill on the Mexico's shrimp fisheries. I flew down to Mexico assuming that the Mexican shrimp industry was a small mom-and-pop operation where fathers passed their boats on to their sons much like in the New England fisheries. I was instantly disabused of this cultural bias as we drove into the bustling coastal city of Mérida. There sitting prominently in the city square was a twenty-five-foot-high bronze statue of a shrimp being sprayed with curtains of splashing water. It turned out that shrimping was second largest industry in Mexico after the oil industry, and that most of the shrimp boats were owned by international businesses who could make back the $600,000 investment in their boats in less than six months. The Iktoc spill represented a battle between two Mexico's two main industries, shrimp and oil.

The international press had been led to believe that the spill had occurred on a Mexican offshore oil platform. But things didn't add up. I was one of the first photographers to arrive, and while I was filming the burning rig from a helicopter, I happened to notice a small decal of an American flag affixed to the porthole of the platform. Later, at the airport, I heard one of the roustabouts who had been rescued from the rig talking about flying back to his cabin in Colorado. Shortly after we left, the damaged rig was hauled out to deeper water and sunk. But what had an American flag and an American oil worker been doing on a Mexican oil rig?

Back in Massachusetts, people were up in arms because a consortium of major oil companies was seeking permission to drill an exploratory well on Georges Bank, one of the world's most productive fishing grounds, located just off New England's coast. The oil companies assured the public that a spill like the one that had occurred in Mexico could never happen on an American rig drilling an exploratory well. I wrote several articles for New England papers, pointing out that the spill *had* occurred on an American rig and it *had* happened while drilling an exploratory well. I had been the first writer to figure out that the rig had actually been owned by an American consortium, even though the incriminating evidence had been hastily sunk in several hundred fathoms of water. The well-hidden fact became a national issue when it was discovered that the then Vice-President George Bush senior had been one of the owners of the rig. I had my first scoop, and wanted more.

Shallow Waters (1979–1980)

Deep-sea mineral mining had been one of the major issues facing the Law of the Sea conference in 1974. Environmentalists had believed that the world's industrial powers were about to start strip mining the ocean floor for manganese nodules: baseball-sized concretions of minerals like copper, nickel, cobalt, and iron. Military planners wanted the minerals because of their strategic value as weapons, and reform-minded internationalists wanted revenues gained from licensing the industrialists as an independent source of revenue to help support the United Nations peacekeeping activities. I was put in the awkward position of having to argue both sides, because half of my salary was paid by the Sierra Club, who wanted to prevent strip-mining the ocean floor and the other half by a Quaker group, who wanted to mine as much as possible to raise money for the United Nations!

The situation was made all the more urgent because by June 1974, the billionaire Howard Hughes was in the Pacific about to start slurping up manganese nodules off the ocean floor and nobody knew what the environmental effects would be. A year earlier, Howard Hughes had commissioned the construction of the *Glomar Explorer,* a sophisticated mining vessel designed specifically to mine for manganese nodules. The ship had been built under tight security in a Baltimore shipyard, and planes had been prevented from flying over it both during construction and as it steamed down the East Coast, and through the Panama Canal into the Pacific. As we were debating, Hughes was preparing to mine.

This had been an extremely hot topic in research circles. I don't know how many hundred-page papers I read about Howard Hughes and manganese nodules. They were written by some of the world's most knowledgeable international lawyers and economists, but none of the papers quite made sense. Nobody knew exactly where Howard Hughes was going to smelt his ore or precisely how he would sell it on the international market. But because he was Howard Hughes, everyone figured he had a trick up his sleeve and was going to make a fortune.

What we didn't know was that the whole project was actually a cover for an elaborate CIA operation to raise a sunken Soviet submarine. The Jennifer Project would become known in spying circles as the CIA's most successful covert operation of all times. Manganese nodules and Howard Hughes were the perfect cover for the operation. The Feds had Hughes over a barrel because he owed several million dollars in back taxes, and he was universally known to be so paranoid that nobody would question the intense security surrounding his mining operations, and manganese nodules were so new that nobody knew much about them anyway. The CIA even trained two crews: one to actually mine for manganese nodules, the other to raise the Soviet sub.

The real story wasn't revealed until 1975, when the *New York Times,* the *L.A. Times,* and the *Washington Post* ran front-page articles that outlined the operation, but explained it had been another dismal failure. The sub had broken in two, and the CIA had only been able to retrieve a small section of the bow. But that was the backup cover story. In fact, the CIA had raised the entire submarine, put it into an underwater barge, blown out the water, and entered the sub, retrieving a trove of materials including codes, nuclear-tipped torpedoes, textbooks that covered the Soviet's entire graduate training program in nuclear engineering, and the bodies of forty-five Soviet sailors. The CIA even performed an official Russian burial-at-sea ceremony and filmed the sailors being dumped back overboard, in case the Soviets made a stink about the desecration of the bodies of the Soviet sailors. But the U.S.S.R. was in no position to make a stink: It had just been caught red-handed with nuclear-tipped torpedoes it had been claiming didn't exist, and the Soviets were certainly not going to advertise the fact that the CIA had been able to use the Soviets' own codes to decipher over six years worth of recorded messages between the Kremlin and its fleet of nuclear submarines.

I, as well as hundreds of the world's most astute lawyers, scientists, and journalists, had been duped into helping to create the false cover through our earnest deliberations and writing. It was a lesson I would remember in future years.

The complete story of the operation came out in a little-known book called *The Jennifer Project*. I happened to stumble across the book in 1977 and decided that the incident could be the basis for a fascinating novel. I spent the summer writing a proposal for a thriller that switched the story to the East Coast and told it through the eyes of a naive young Woods Hole scientist who thought she was being hired to study plankton aboard a research vessel designed to mine the ocean floor. *Thresher* included lots of action, several steamy sex scenes, and featured at least two Chinese agents being drowned in Woods Hole's peaceful Eel Pond. So I had a book proposal but no idea how to get a publisher or agent.

In 1978 an ad agency had called to ask if I would like to be in an ad for "The kind of man who reads *Playboy* magazine." They wanted to feature my exploits on American and Soviet vessels, but of course they also wanted to exploit the fact that my father had been the Republican governor of Massachusetts from 1969 to 1975. I explained that I had never actually read *Playboy,* just looked at the pictures. They didn't seem to care. Of course, my mother was appalled, claiming she donated money to stop such trash! But my father was mildly amused and thought a little publicity couldn't hurt. In the end, the ads appeared in major newspapers throughout the country. I had happened to mention in the ad that I was working on a novel about a CIA plot to raise a Soviet submarine. In no time flat, a literary agent was on the phone asking if he could represent me. Sometimes drastic measures have to be taken to get into the publishing world. I don't necessarily advocate that aspiring writers try to appear in an ad for *Playboy* magazine, but if the opportunity arises . . .

My agent shopped the proposal around to all the major houses, but the trouble with fiction is that you have to write the entire book first. With nonfiction, usually all you have to do is write three sample chapters and an outline. So I had an agent, but no book. Plus, I had discovered that I couldn't really write in a woman's voice, and was frankly having trouble taking my novel seriously. Most of all, I was not writing about what was really important to me. I was not writing naturally.

I don't necessarily advocate that a young writer appear in an ad for *Playboy* magazine, but if the opportunity arises . . . *Photo by Steve Brosnahan.*

My opportunity to write naturally came about in an unexpected way. I happened to bump into a friend in Harvard Square who was about to make a film about a freshwater pond for the newly formed *NOVA* science series. He asked if I would like to be a consultant on the project. I had to admit I didn't know anything about freshwater ponds but suggested that after he was done making the pond film, I had one they could make about a saltwater estuary. A year later, Peace River Films called back. The film company was considering making a film about either the Parker River estuary north of Boston or Pleasant Bay on Cape Cod. I lobbied hard for the Cape Cod location, showing the filmmakers all our research and the thousands of underwater photos that Ken Read had taken to chronicle the bay. At that time, everyone had already seen photos of coral reefs but few people had bothered to take pictures of northern marine animals, which were largely unknown but I think more interesting.

Peace River also wanted to produce a companion book to its estuary film. It had already approached John McPhee, who was known for his books and articles in *The New Yorker,* and Bill MacLeish, editor of *Oceanus* magazine in Woods Hole. I had spent ten years of my life researching and photographing Pleasant Bay. I wasn't about to give it all away. Elbows flew. Finally I was given permission to present a separate proposal to Houghton Mifflin, which was accepted. Both Houghton Mifflin and *NOVA* wanted me to write a companion book to the film, but Peace River didn't want to be distracted by having to take still photos. I ended up doing both the photography and the writing for the book. *Shallow Waters* was never advertised as a companion book to a *NOVA* film, which would have helped national sales. But it didn't really matter. I had a contract, and we started to film in February. It was a wonderful year. We spent every day either diving in the bay, flying over it in a plane, or skimming over its surface in boats.

Neil Goodwin and John Borden were both engineers and loved the challenge of designing systems to come up with the shots they needed. They had already developed a distinct signature, going back and forth between wide-angle establishing shot and close-ups of the most macroscopic of creatures. The macro shots were filmed in tanks, where the tanks, the cameras, and the lights were all suspended on gimbals and could be individually controlled, so the viewer felt like he or she was swimming through the macroscopic world. Sometimes we would mount the camera on a two-by-four projecting off the bow of my boat and lower it into the water by pulleys as the boat skimmed down a narrow creek between towering rows of seed-laden *Spartina* grass. The following scene would cut to a tank shot, but it would open with the same downward motion so the two shots fit seamlessly together. Even though I had been driving the boat and knew the photographers had switched from a wide-angle lens to a macroscopic shot,

I believed the fiction that the camera had panned underwater in one long continuous shot.

We filmed the intimate lives of plankton, herring, horseshoe crabs, and terns as they entered the bay, laid eggs, and migrated back out in the fall. I did the same thing in my book, presenting the chapters as a series of experiences—diving with plankton, watching stickleback and pipefish, going out at night to observe spawning horseshoe crabs, and hiding in blinds to witness nesting terns.

There was a method to my madness. Just before I started my book, a friend from Harvard's anthropology department had told me about a new book that codified the gene thinking we had discovered as undergraduates: "You have to read this book. You will never look at animal behavior the same way again." She was right. *Sex Evolution and Behavior,* written by Martin Daly and Margo Wilson, showed that individual animals pursue different strategies because of the mathematics behind sexual selection. Males have the ability to father hundreds of offspring, so it makes genetic sense for them to be promiscuous, while females can only produce a limited number of offspring, so it makes genetic sense for them to be choosy in selecting a mate who will be a good provider. It makes sense for older and younger siblings to have different strategies to vie for their parents' investment.

Sometimes these parental investment situations were not so pretty, like when adult terns starve younger chicks in order to ensure the survival of older chicks in which they have already made a substantial parental investment. It seemed cruel, but in terms of the mathematics of parental investment it made sense. When human parents have to make snap judgments about which child to save in horrific situations like the recent tsunami in the Indian Ocean, how many of them sacrifice the lives of their youngest children in order to save their oldest?

So although I presented my story as a simple ramble through the seasons, it was also carefully designed to reveal the sexual strategies of each species as I worked my way up through the animal kingdom. I paid particular attention to phenomena like the pseudo-pregnancy of male pipefish. In these fish the female lays her eggs in a special pouch on the male's abdomen. The male is left brooding the eggs while the female goes off promiscuously courting other males. It is the exception that proves the rule that the parent who invests the most effort into raising offspring is selected to be more monogamous, and the parent who invests the least is selected to be more polygamous. It doesn't matter whether the individual parents happen to be male or female, although in most species physiology dictates that it is the female who becomes pregnant and tend to be more monogamous. In other words, if we could find a way for males to become pregnant we would expect the sexual strategies of the sexes to reverse, as they do in the pipefish.

It was in the midst of writing *Shallow Waters* that I discovered the true importance of chapter outlines. When I had originally written the chapter outline, it had only seemed like part of the process to get a contract. But I discovered how important the chapter outline is when you are in the middle of your book and you have just finished a chapter and have no idea what you should do next. That's when you pull out your chapter outline and see what you wrote when you were thinking about the structure of the entire book, not just the individual chapters. Nine times out of ten, your original outline tells you exactly where to go next.

It was also during that summer that I discovered I could only focus on doing one thing at a time. Some days, I would concentrate on helping to make the film; other days, I would concentrate on taking still photographs or simply go out and take notes for my book. But when I tried to do two things at once, neither came out right.

Toward the end of the summer I stepped on a razor clam and had to have ten stitches sewn into the ball of my foot. I kept on working, with one foot bare and the other in a sandal to keep my bandages dry. It was just enough to throw my back out of kilter, but I didn't realize what was happening at the time. We were lifting heavy camera equipment in and out of boats, and after a few days I thought I was getting a kidney infection because I had a pain deep within my body, near my spine. By November I could barely get out of bed and decided I had to see a doctor. He gave me mega doses of valium and the news that I had herniated a disc. I would have to have surgery on my back and be bedridden for several months. I was stunned and asked my publishers for an extension on my deadline, but they replied, "No book, no contract." I ended up writing most of the book while lying flat on my back in the Massachusetts General Hospital. In many ways this

The author and his father standing in Pleasant Bay. *Photo by Jessie Sargent.*

helped with my discipline. I fell into the routine of writing two or three hours a day, every day, seven days a week.

By the time my book came out in June 1980, I was feeling my mortality. It was my thirty-fifth birthday. I was in the middle of a divorce, and my father had just suffered a major heart attack. But my editor called to say that *Publisher's Weekly* had just compared *Shallow Waters* to the writings of Lewis Thomas and Stephen Jay Gould. I didn't bother to walk on the earth for the next few weeks.

The book had been helped by coming out at exactly the right time. The environmental movement was in full swing, and I had tried to use the most up-to-date thinking in both animal behavior and ecology while still keeping the writing simple and readable. Major publishers had been looking for books that used the latest science to investigate ecology in their readers' own backyards. Even without the imprimatur of the *NOVA* Science Series, *Shallow Waters* won the *Boston Globe*'s Winship award and sold well throughout the country. In those days, national publishers were looking for books about specific areas. Today the large booksellers that buy in quantity have convinced publishers that such books should only be marketed as regional books, so regional publishers have filled the niche formerly filled by major houses.

But I was hooked. After all those years, I had finally found something I could do reasonably well. My agent wanted another book, my publisher wanted another book, I wanted another book. Now all I had to do was find a subject.

Confessions of a Horseshoe Crab Farmer (1980–1982)

My editor at Houghton Mifflin, Daphne Abeel, had a reputation as a *bête noir* within the publishing world. Just before signing my contract Daphne asked, "So, Bill, just how strong is your marriage?" This is probably a question that should be asked of more first-time authors. Few people realize how preoccupied a writer will become with his work.

My marriage to Claudia Praeger started to drift apart in 1979. She chose to remain on Martha's Vineyard while I moved to Cape Cod to finish the *NOVA* film. In the early days of our marriage, we had often rented out our house in Cambridge so we could afford to spend our summers in Claudia's parents' house on the Vineyard. It was where I

Author shot for *Shallow Waters: A Year on Cape Cod's Pleasant Bay*. *Photo by Jessie Sargent.*

had done most of the work on my proposal for the Howard Hughes novel about raising a Soviet sub. At the beginning of those summers, I would write from nine to four in the afternoon before going to the nude beach for a swim. By the end of the summer, I was only writing from nine to eleven before the beach lured me away.

Actually, Lucy Vincent Beach was where most of the real business of publishing was done. Most of New York's best writers, publishers, and agents would be standing about stark naked, pitching ideas and making deals. I remember swimming with Carly Simon and Frank Rich while commenting on the rear end of Alan Dershowitz as he practiced arguing a case. The culmination of those years was the birth of our son Ben, a talented artist now making his own decisions about choosing stability or the artistic life.

But working on the *NOVA* film was a turning point. I had to put the the fun and frivolousness of the Vineyard behind me in order to concentrate on my writing. I came back a different person. It was painful for all of us when I finally decided to leave.

There was excitement in the air about presenting science to the public in the eighties. The environmental movement had inspired some of the older nature journals like *The Smithsonian* and *Natural History Magazine* to expand their readership. Many new magazines like *OMNI* and *Discover* catered to the public's new interest in science. But programs like *NOVA* and *Nature* had also shown that not only was there a large national audience for science, but television was the best way to reach it. A few people even thought there could be a market for science programming beyond public television. One of those people was Robert Guccionni, the publisher of *Penthouse* magazine. Guccionni had just launched *OMNI* magazine. It was selling briskly, and he wanted to expand into television.

Guccionni approached PBS about the idea of producing a magazine-style television program that would present four short science pieces per program instead of *NOVA*'s hour-long single-subject format. Public television turned him down flat, but he convinced two of the producers of *NOVA* to spin off a new company to try his idea on network television. Graham Chedd and David Angier decided to hire four unknown new hosts to present different topics for their *OMNI* series. They asked me if I would like to host the underwater segments. Actually they gave me two choices, either walk through a burning building in an experimental new asbestos fire-retardant suit, or dive under an ice floe in a SCUBA tank. I chose the latter. We drove down to Woods Hole, where I swam beneath the ice, then rose up through a hole in the floe, spitting out a mouthful of salty water before spitting out my lines. I still remember the discordance between the noisy clutter on the surface and the quiet, greenish calm beneath the world of ice. Chedd-Angier shot other segments at Cape Canaveral and in the Massachusetts General Hospital in Boston. Their final demo was a dramatic mélange of space shots, underwater photography, experimental bicycles, and bypass surgery.

OMNI and later Carl Sagan's *COSMOS* proved to be great successes on network television. In those days most cities only had access to three major network stations and PBS, so the entire country knew when a significant new science series was about to air. I am still convinced that television is one of the best vehicles to present science to a large audience. But today, few companies will support the kind of intelligent science series that existed in the eighties. If they did, nobody would be able to find them in the morass of shows about eating bugs and catching venomous snakes. On television, nature has reverted back to being dangerous and unsavory, something that should be overcome and subdued, not something to be understood and appreciated. Sadly, this weakens the environmental movement at precisely the moment when we need the movement the most.

A month before we were scheduled to start shooting the series, Guccionni pulled the contract from Chedd–Angier and hired Walter Cronkite to replace us as hosts! Chedd–Angier was stunned. It had been their demo that had sold the show to Guccionni's advertisers. I was beginning to understand the fickle nature of television. And I was in a familiar situation: I was broke and facing the prospect of spending the summer alone and unemployed. Sexless in the city.

My only consolation from the entire fiasco was that the new producer of the series told me that the piece that I had suggested about horseshoe crabs had received the most responses of any of their stories. It had featured a boy whose life was saved from spinal meningitis after being diagnosed with horseshoe crab blood. The piece stressed that no crabs were killed in the bleeding process. But I was beginning to have my doubts. When we had collected crabs for the Marine Biological Laboratory, the crabs were often returned to us dead or dying. I decided there might be an interesting story there and that the only way to get accurate information was to go undercover and collect crabs from Associates of Cape Cod, the company that was bleeding the crabs commercially.

Nineteen eighty-two turned out to be an eventful summer. I met my future wife Kristina Lindborg, who was directing the news for our local Cape Cod radio station. I remembered her voice from the days when she had worked for Monitor radio in Boston. I convinced her to come see our jolly crew of horseshoe crab collectors—Tom Gedaminski, a student of mine at Boston College, and John Dinga, former curator of the Baltimore Aquarium. John had told me he could get horseshoe crabs from Delaware Bay, where they were bigger and more plentiful than those from Pleasant Bay. The president of Associates of

Cape Cod couldn't wait to get his hands on the larger crabs. But we all neglected one thing. The FDA had a requirement that the crabs be returned to the water from which they came. Needless to say, everything went wrong that summer. Trucks broke down, we had to retrieve crabs from Woods Hole's holding pools just before a site visit by the admiral of the Navy's Office of Naval Research, and several crabs were released back into Pleasant Bay.

But I also discovered that under industrial conditions as many as 50 percent of the crabs sometimes died, and that the large needles used for bleeding would often come back to us still inserted in the crabs' carapaces. In the end I blew the whistle on myself, explaining to the town shellfish constable what we had done and warning him to tighten up the town's regulations. The story got into the local newspaper under the headline "Author of *Shallow Waters* in Hot Water," and the story spread to several Boston papers. I was quite rightfully criticized as an environmentalist gone wrong.

After the summer was over, I decided to write *Confessions of a Horseshoe Crab Farmer,* a book about our troubles raising horseshoe crabs. I tried to write the proposal in the humorous style of some of the European nature writers like Gerald Durrell and Konrad Lorenz. But I discovered that American publishers don't want amusing stories about natural history. My editor at W. W. Norton finally convinced me to write a serious book about how marine animals like horseshoe crabs, lobsters, and squid are used in modern medicine.

I literally followed our crabs back to Woods Hole to write the book. But this time I had a track record. My first book had received such positive reviews that I felt like I had to measure up. So instead of writing naturally, I kept worrying about all the Woods Hole scientists looking over my shoulder. I forgot that my job was to write for the public, not for scientific approval.

Still, writing *The Year of the Crab* became a fascinating experience. Simply by concentrating on marine animals used in research, I was able to describe some of the major milestones in modern medicine. I had never taken a course in biomedical history, however, so I stayed very close to the original research papers. I didn't want to oversimplify anything or make any embarrassing gaffes, so my first draft was fairly technical. When I handed it in, I expected that my editor

The author as happy horseshoe crab farmer. *Photo by Sarah Bacon.*

would have me rewrite and smooth out large portions of the manuscript. But he never did. It was a little like getting a B+ on a paper—you don't go to your teacher and ask if you can have your paper back so you can rewrite it to get an A. At least I never did.

But people still show up at book signings clutching worn copies of *The Year of the Crab,* claiming that it is their favorite book of all time. I guess there is just no accounting for taste. I still find it overblown, stilted, and idiosyncratic—but at least I had gotten my second book out of the way. There is a little-known secret in publishing circles that second books are notoriously difficult to write. Authors have usually been thinking about their first books for most of their lives. But second books sneak up on you and you just have to get them out of the way so you can concentrate on your third and fourth books!

Woods Hole (1981–1990)

By autumn, the money we had made from collecting horseshoe crabs was dwindling fast. Kristina and I had decided that we would stay on the Cape so we could both continue to report and write about what we knew best. Fortunately, I had been offered a job teaching at the SEA program in Woods Hole. It was only a six-week, temporary job, but it would give us the start we needed.

It would also allow me to teach a writing course that I had been thinking about for years. Here was a group of college-educated science students about to board a tall ship for a six-week oceanographic cruise to the Caribbean. I wanted to prepare them for writing about this potentially life changing experience. I found that most of the students were eager to take the course. They had yet to be socialized into thinking that there should be a rigid separation between science and the humanities. They still felt you could be a good scientist and write for the public as well. Many of them told me that this was exactly the kind of course they had been searching for.

I had them read passages from *The Voyage of the Beagle,* a book written by Charles Darwin, who sailed aboard the *Beagle* when he was the same age as my students, and passages from the log of the *Challenger Expedition,* generally considered to be the first oceanographic research cruise and the event that ushered in the new field of oceanog-

Bill and Kristina in Woods Hole.

raphy. They also read *The Open Ocean* by Sir Alister Hardy and *The Log From the Voyage to the Sea of Cortez,* a classic piece of natural history writing by the inestimable John Steinbeck. Then I sent them into the field to simply sit and observe the plants, animals, and geology of the area. Later I had them visit colonies of cormorants and seals to write about animal behavior. The first location I chose for a lab session was on the cold, wet sand of Nobska Beach, where a sunfish was sitting half buried in the sand. The *Mola mola* is a large fish that has enormous eyes and swims on the surface, sluggishly feeding on jellyfish. It also has a large, floppy pectoral fin that flaps in the air so people often mistake it for a shark. But the most salient feature of the fish is that it looks like it should be ten feet longer than it is. It is almost all head with a stumpy tail, which in this specimen was conveniently buried under the sand. It was the perfect mystery fish. I doubted the students would unearth the tail to make the correct identification without some urging. So I gave the students Bigelow and Schroeder's *Fishes of the Gulf of Maine,* the classic book of fish identification. Bigelow and Schroeder has a biological key that allows you to identify a specimen by carefully choosing between specific features. It might start by asking a broad question like, does your fish have bones or cartilage; then if it has cartilage the key directs you to the shark family, where it asks you more specific questions, until you finally have your identification.

This seemed like the perfect assignment. We had a big, rare, mysterious fish sitting unidentified in the sand. I figured my students would learn how to use a key, and be encouraged to observe nature more closely. Unfortunately, I happened to mention the project to a young man walking on the beach. Of course I didn't realize he would be starting the course the following day and would tell the whole class that we would be identifying a *Mola mola!* But the process, not the answer, was the point.

I started by having the students visit and write about beaches, marshes, and forests. Later I had them visit labs, attend lectures, and interview scientists. Many of the students had already had fascinating experiences, and the course gave them the opportunity to write about those experiences for the first time.

One student was living with a Woods Hole family whose father had Alzheimer's disease. He wrote a moving essay about the effects of the disease on the entire family, then shifted to a detailed description of what was known about the etiology of the disease and how it affects the brain's proteins and synapses. It was a masterful piece, written before many articles about Alzheimer's had appeared in the mainstream press. Another student was a former summer ranger at Yellowstone National Park. He wrote a lyrical piece about hiking into a remote corner of the park and spending all day waiting for a geyser to blow. A student who had studied sociology wrote a Veblinesque piece about conspicuous consumption and Cape Cod's lawns. An adventurous young woman went undercover to write a chilling piece about the drug culture of Woods Hole. I realized how fresh and spontaneous their writing still was and how important it is to get to future scientists before they are taught the wrong way to write.

Woods Hole was the perfect place to teach such a course. Here was a whole community dedicated to unlocking the secrets of nature. I had experienced Woods Hole when I had debarked from the village on the *Atlantis II* and the *Belegorsk*. But these had been cruises sponsored by the Woods Hole Oceanographic Institution and the National Marine Fisheries Service. These institutions had the boats and the research that was so well known to the public. But I soon learned that the more interesting stories lurked just down the street in the Marine Biological Laboratory. In scientific circles, the MBL is the most prestigious of all the Woods Hole institutions. Every summer, hundreds of the world's best biologists descend on the MBL to study animals like horseshoe crabs, lobster, and squid. In the process they have made some of the most important discoveries in modern medicine. Over forty of the scientists have won Nobel prizes for their efforts. Even Gertrude Stein spent a summer here when she was in medical school. Perhaps that is where she came up with the objectivity of "a rose, is a rose, is a rose."

We had very little money in those days. Most of our protein came from catching bluefish off the WHOI docks and diving for bluecrabs on our daily swims. We would skin-dive every day from April to November to look for the crabs, and the experience made me realize how much you could learn from diving every day in the same location. I used the experience to describe the change of seasons underwater in subsequent books.

In the spring we would go down to the docks, where the commercial fishermen would give you as much squid as you could carry home. Our dog grew to hate the guts of squid; which was all we could afford to feed him until the summer arrived. One day my son Ben and I were fishing on the Cape Cod Canal when we noticed that big fat red lobster bodies were floating by in the water below us. They were being pitched out of the back window of a nearby restaurant. We could hear the cooks inside happily chopping the boiled lobsters in two, before chucking the bodies out the window because the restaurant only served lobster tails. We scooped up the bodies and continued to enjoy delicious lobster dinners whenever we fished in what became our favorite spot.

But we were not alone. Nobody had very much money in Woods Hole in the eighties. A few scientists drew regular salaries, but most scientists lived primarily off the soft money they received from continually applying for research grants. One group of oceanographers broke away from the established institutions to start a nonprofit organization that charged far less overhead on grants than the other organizations. They asked me if I would like to join. This was the opportunity that I had been waiting for. It would allow me to combine all my interests under one roof. I established the Coastlines Project to promote books, articles, and films about coastal issues. My long-term project was to create a television series about the marshes, beaches, and estuaries that I loved.

My first project was to approach the *Cape Cod Times* about writing a weekly column on coastal issues. This was pretty much a slam-dunk proposition because just about everything on Cape Cod was a coastal issue. I grew to love that weekly assignment. It gave me license to write about almost anything I wanted. Scientists often ask me the best way they can use their knowledge to influence public policy. I tell them to write regularly for their local newspaper, whether it be the *New York Times* or their hometown rag. Books come and go and articles in scientific journals are seldom seen. The only way to really reach the public is to meet the public in the marketplace of ideas, and for most people that continues to be their daily newspaper.

Kristina was producing news stories for Cape Cod's leading radio station. Soon she received a call from the *Christian Science Monitor.*

We would skin-dive in Woods Hole every day from April to December. I realized how much you could learn from diving in the same spot every day throughout the seasons. *Photo by Kristina Sargent.*

Ben and I photograph birds at the Ding Darling Sanctuary in Sanibel, Florida. *Photo by Jessie Sargent.*

They were expanding into shortwave radio and needed worldwide news coverage. They hired Kristina to cover national and international topics, and I sent them a tape of one of the programs I had produced for Cape Cod radio. Eventually they hired me to produce *The Science Spot*, a weekly science series they broadcast to Asia, Europe, South America, and Africa. Radio is an incredibly powerful medium, and it is still the most influential medium in the Third World. I wrote the stories during the week and drove to Boston to record them. It is amazing what you can do with music, sound effects, and good writing. One week I took my readers a mile underwater to listen to whales, and the next week we visited Jupiter. I covered everything from nuclear energy, to drilling through the ice in Antarctica, to the use of horseshoe crabs in modern medicine. I followed birds migrating from Tierra del Fuego to the Arctic Circle, and the trajectory of nuclear missiles as they left the Soviet Union and rained down on North America to create a nuclear winter. For just a few thousand dollars you could take your audience to the depths of the ocean or deep into space, something that was prohibitively expensive to do on film. We received letters from around the world, but my favorite rebuked me with, "You silly goose, don't you know that crabs can't possibly have ten eyes?"

After a few years, Monitor radio moved into television and asked me if I would do a science show for it. I still had my films of the Soviet fishing fleet, the Iktoc oil spill, and natural history shots of everything from whales to terns to horseshoe crabs. It was also amazing how easy it was to get existing footage of things like rocket launches and artists' depictions of planetary fly-bys. Every week we located footage, lined up guests, and prepared a discussion of the implications of the week's main scientific events. Soon I knew when satellites were going to rendezvous with distant planets and when Congressional hearings were going to be held on different topics. It was an adrenaline rush to gear yourself up so you could speak about the week's most significant science events, whether they be in ecology, medicine, or space travel. It was also amazing how many letters I got from old friends who I never would have thought spent that much time watching television!

Of all these media, I found that it was radio that improved my writing the most. Because I was writing something that had to be read, I would read it aloud to make sure that it sounded just right. I often found myself making hand gestures to explain significant points. Now I find it almost impossible to explain a difficult concept without waving my hands in the air while I write. I call it the Bellarinni School of Science Writing, named after my great-grandmother, Eva Bellarinni.

These radio habits helped make my writing snappier and more colloquial. In my earlier writing I had tried to express the magnificence of nature, but radio taught me to lighten up. Magnificence is great, but science can also be amusing and a lot of fun.

During these years, several publishers asked me to write books. The good thing about having a publisher approach you is that they generally have a pretty marketable idea. I, unfortunately, was becoming known for books that were famously difficult to market. The other good thing about being approached by publishers is that they generally pay pretty better and more quickly for their own ideas than for yours. I ended up writing the text for *The Undersea Life of America*, a beautiful coffee table book that explored the coasts of America, and *Night Reef*, a children's book about what goes on on a coral reef after dark.

All of these assignments were enjoyable, and well paid. But I was looking forward to getting deeply immersed in another one of my unmarketable books about a tiny peculiar subject—this one would be about an inlet!

Chapter 4

Writing Naturally

Storm Surge

On January 2, 1987, a midwinter storm burst through the barrier beach that protects Pleasant Bay. It was like permanently breaching the levees of New Orleans. Cold Atlantic waters rushed directly through the new inlet, making the bay six inches higher at high tide and six inches lower at low tide. They continue to do so twenty years later. Overnight, the citizens of Chatham, Massachusetts, had to face the amount of sea-level rise that most communities won't face in fifty years. One hundred and twenty houses were put in jeopardy, half a dozen people lost their homes, and Chatham's lucrative fishing industry almost went kaput. Here was the perfect case study to investigate the effects of sea-level rise. I jumped at the chance to write about this global issue affecting my own backyard.

From the beginning, I knew I was not going to be a totally objective bystander. I had grown up on Pleasant Bay, studied it for several decades, and had already written two books about it.

My first reaction was excitement. As a Cape Cod kid, I have always loved hurricanes. Writing this book would give me the chance to chronicle both the short-term effects of this storm and the long-term effects of sea-level rise.

Nauset Beach, the barrier beach that protects Chatham, has one of the most powerful sand transport systems on our planet. Every year, longshore currents move the equivalent of a dozen football fields filled eight feet high with sand along this beach, and every year Nauset grows 200 to 300 feet, or about a mile every ten years. The process is so dramatic that it can even be seen from space. An astronaut sitting on Mars would be able to see these geological changes.

My second reaction was smug satisfaction. Some of the buildings that shouldn't have been built so near the water in the first place would now be washed away so the beach could revert to its natural condition. My early articles reflected this, the prevailing environmental ethic that coastal communities should gradually retreat in the face of sea-level rise.

One prominent environmental author even advocated that the government should step in and remove all buildings within a mile of the oceans. The prospect didn't please her neighbors on Martha's Vineyard, nor the millions of people in major coastal cities like Boston, New York, Baltimore, Miami, or New Orleans. On reflection, I realized that since college I had never lived more than a mile from the ocean. Neither, I think, had the author, with her island houses on Manhattan and Martha's Vineyard!

My third reaction came when I realized that my parents' house, situated twelve miles away from the inlet, was also going to be affected by the new higher tides. I began to battle the state to get permission to build a rock-filled revetment to protect my boyhood home. Suddenly I was thrust into a world of draconian regulations and unfair policy implementation. I grew to become ashamed of my former cavalier attitude about people's homes being swept away for the benefit of the environment. I realized that losing one's home is a traumatic event that will reverberate through a family for generations. One only has to look at people being forced from their homes by natural events like Hurricane Katrina or man-made events like the evacuation of the Gaza strip to realize the extent of their loss. Territoriality is hard-wired into our psyches. Psychologists rank being forced from your home as being almost as traumatic as experiencing divorce or a death in the family.

I started to think the unthinkable. What if the numbers were wrong? What if society had promulgated regulations based on shaky science? I looked into the history of forecasting sea-level rise. In 1980 Dr. Stephen Schneider published a paper that showed that global warming would cause the oceans to rise twenty-eight feet in the next 100 years. Less official papers had put the number closer to a hundred feet per century. The media had scooped up these reports and repeated them with flashy graphics of waves lapping over the top of the Statue of Liberty and the Washington monument. Much less attention was paid when Dr. Schneider quietly retracted the numbers in a tiny footnote on a back page of *Scientific American*. He said, in effect, "Oops, I made a mistake, poor math. Actually the oceans will only rise twelve feet in the next century." From there the numbers dropped precipitously from twelve feet, to six feet, to three feet of sea-level rise in the next 100 years. Now most scientists agree that the oceans will only rise from six to eighteen inches in the next century, approximately the same amount that the oceans rose in the past century. Not the end of the world, but certainly enough to cause mischief like we were witnessing in Chatham, and the floods that would soon drown New Orleans.

But the die was cast. Most of the environmental regulations governing coastal erosion had been drafted during the years when scientists still believed that the oceans were going to rise thirty feet per century. Massachusetts had enacted one of the first and most comprehensive wetlands protection regulations in the country. But the regulation included what was termed the dune-bank distinction. According to this distinction, if it was determined that your house was built on a coastal bank, you could go ahead and build a seawall to protect your home. But if your house was built on a coastal dune you could not. This appeared to make sense, as most dunes were on migratory barrier beaches where it didn't make sense to build a house.

But what about the mainland? In places like Cape Cod, the coasts alternated back and forth between coastal banks and coastal dunes. Instead of just banning the construction of homes on barrier beaches the way other states had done, Massachusetts came up with the dune–bank distinction. But the trouble with the dune–bank distinction was how it was determined. The only way a state official could tell whether your house was on a coastal bank or a dune was to scoop a handful of sand from below your house, take it back to the lab, and look at it under a microscope. If the sand grains were under a certain size it was determined that your house was on a coastal bank; if the sand grains were over a certain size it was determined that your house was on a coastal dune. This seemed like a pretty fine distinction if your house was on the line.

The distinction also led to some ludicrous situations. In Chatham, it was determined that the town could build a seawall to protect a parking lot and that the Chatham Beach and Tennis Club could build a seawall to protect its tennis courts, but that Bert Nelson, a homeowner immediately adjacent to both the tennis courts and the parking lot, could do nothing to protect his million-dollar home.

Actually, the state relented and allowed Mr. Nelson to spend $30,000 to renourish the beach in front of his house. The sand was washed away in less than fifteen minutes in the second random storm. Then the state said Mr. Nelson could spend $50,000 to build a temporary sandbag seawall to protect his home. This was washed away in the third random storm. Finally it said Mr. Nelson could spend $150,000 to move his house back thirty feet, where it would be considered to be on a coastal bank, so then he could build a seawall. In all Mr. Nelson spent over $450,000 in legal and engineering fees, and by 1993 he had less than nineteen feet of sand in front of his house. It looked like it would be washed away during the winter. And what happened? The inlet moved naturally south and by spring 1994, Mr. Nelson had over 300 feet of new beach sand in front of his house. It still protects his home.

I also realized that many of the assumptions that environmentalists held about the negative effects of sea-level rise were also suspect. Scientists had predicted that if the sea level rose more than half an inch over a year, the marshes would start to drown. But Pleasant Bay was now six inches higher than before and the marshes appeared to be thriving. In fact, the productivity of the clam flats had risen so dramatically since the inlet opened that the employment rate had increased by half a percent. Now close to 200 fishermen who had been unemployed or flipping hamburgers for minimum wage were making a good living digging for soft-shelled clams in new shellfish beds created by the changed currents.

This was an eye-opener. At least some of these positive changes would be seen in other communities hit with sea-level rise. This was new information that was not being discussed in forums on global warming. I hoped I could do something about it.

But I also realized that articles could not fully convey the complexity of everything that was happening in Chatham. There was a book to be written, but first I had to convince someone to publish it. Who was going to publish a book about an inlet?

My agent filled my head with images of the movie that could be made and shopped my proposal to all the major houses. But finally Jack McCrae, a long time editor at Henry Holt Company, took me aside and confided, "You know I like this book a lot, but frankly, you will do a lot better with it if you go with a regional press. We can only afford to give this kind of book a few weeks of publicity, but a regional press will stick with it for years." It was a revelation to hear this from a major publisher, but it was also not altogether a surprise. I knew the book would be considered a local book even though I felt it would provide valuable lessons for other communities. I didn't realize how similar Chatham's story would be to that of New Orleans almost twenty years later.

Parnassus Press on Cape Cod had always been my back-up. It had already published the paperback edition of *Shallow Waters* and was busy carving out a niche for itself publishing new and old books about Cape Cod. The press's authors included such luminaries as Thoreau and Henry Beston. I realized it should have been my first choice, not my last.

Parnassus picked up my book, and it was a delightful change. Houghton Mifflin had been less than enthusiastic about *Shallow Waters* after *NOVA* dropped out of the picture. It took Jim Mairs, my editor at W. W. Norton, several months to convince his colleagues to publish *The Year of the Crab*. A year later he explained why: "All the editors sit in a circle and we present our books one by one. I knew it was going to be hard to sell a book about horseshoe crabs, so I knew I had to wait for several of my other books to be rejected, before it would be my turn again. But I also knew I had an ace up my sleeve. For years I had tried to get my colleagues to pick up a book about corkscrews. Eventually they had felt so sorry for me that they relented. Of course the book turned out to be a great success so I could always say, 'Remember what happened with that book about corkscrews?'"

This time we didn't have to resort to such stratagems. The people at Parnassus were familiar with my column in the *Cape Cod Times* and had been pleased with the success of *Shallow Waters*. From the beginning they were eager to get my book and planned to feature it prominently in their marketing strategy. They also knew something I didn't: Cape Cod is a particularly good place to sell books. During the summer months, all the East Coast reading establishment wants to do is park itself on a Cape Cod beach and read a good book.

Since my experience with Parnassus, I have made a point of pitching all my books to academic and regional publishers who know their market. Each successive book has been a more pleasant experience. Sometimes I miss the ego boost of a good review in the *New York Times,* but it is more than made up for by publishers who stick with your book years after its release.

I had several long, informal sessions with my Parnassus publishers in their Hyannis office. We discussed everything from cover art to titles. Most readers may not realize it, but selecting a title is usually the very last thing you do when writing a book. It is only after you have completed the book that you really know what you have been writing about.

I had been using a frightfully boring working title, and Wally Exman delicately suggested that perhaps something more stimulating might be in order. We argued back and forth, and finally Wally thumbed through my manuscript reading out technical terms as potential titles. He mentioned "storm surge" and we all laughed, as it seemed wildly over the top. But that night I couldn't sleep. "Storm surge" was a little-known technical term that people usually only hear when a hurricane is approaching their home, but the term also conveyed the complexity and power of sea-level rise. News reporters seldom use the term correctly; a storm surge is experienced not as a wave of water but more like a high tide that keeps the sea level above normal levels throughout a hurricane. The next morning I called Wally back to explain why *Storm Surge* was exactly the title we should use. It fit so perfectly that now I can't even remember my old working title.

It sometimes takes several months to convince a publisher to accept your book, so if I feel a book is important enough I often start writing it before a contract comes through. It takes a leap of faith, but it is important to start writing while your idea is hot. Otherwise you might find you have lost interest in the subject by the time your contract comes through. Writing before you have a contract also allows you to improve your manuscript and gives your publisher a better idea of what to expect. By the time I reached Parnassus I had written the entire manuscript as a scientific book, but suddenly I realized this was more of a people story than a science story. I sat down to rewrite *Storm Surge* telling the story through the eyes of the scientists, lawyers, anglers, and homeowners involved.

To get myself into the mood for writing this new kind of book, I wrote an opening chapter that takes place in a local bar. I had people telling their stories in a great big disjointed beery conversation laced with heavy dialects. It was almost like an extended "Bert and I" routine. I had actually written the piece as a writing exercise, fully expecting to discard it. But I found I liked the passage so much that I kept it in the final book, along with a prototypical old Cape Cod fisherman whose wife jabs him in the ribs for farting under the covers. Of course several reviewers took exception to my local stereotypes, but I had grown to like my characters. Besides, sometimes it's good to give your readers a chuckle before hitting them with too much heavy science.

But writing a people story presented several other problems. I couldn't just plunge into a straightforward discussion of something like the dune–bank distinction. I had to introduce it the way the people involved learned about it. The first time the reader hears about the regulation is in an early chapter when a state official scoops up a handful of sand and offhandedly remarks to a companion that it is probably from another dune. A few chapters later, some homeowners are interviewing a potential lawyer about his knowledge of environmental law:

> "What do you know about the dune–bank distinction?"
> "What the hell is that?"
> "Benoit is saying that half the houses are on a dune and the state regulations say you can't build seawalls in front of a dune, but you can in front of a bank."
> "Why, that's absurd! How do they know the difference?"
> "Size of the grains, I guess. How would you argue against it?
> "I'll just say there is not enough sand left."
> "I say let's give him a try. Why not let him go out there and talk to Channel 58?" . . .
> "I didn't know the first thing about the dune–bank distinction," Soutter recalled later. But there is an old saying in trial law, 'when all else fails argue quantity.' So I went out there and went on and on about there not being

enough sand left in front of the houses to tell the difference. Two weeks later the Galanti's cottage was washed away and I looked like a goddamned genius."

I had gleaned the dialogue from listening to the news piece and interviewing both Soutter and homeowners. I felt the passage gave just enough information about the dune–bank distinction and did not interfere with the emotion of the scene. It was only in one of the last chapters of the book that I presented a detailed discussion of the dune–bank distinction.

I tried to write the book artfully, so it would read like a novel but still do justice to the science. I was helped by the inherent drama of the situation. In one chapter I described three people trapped in their shack in the dunes and exhausted from trying to talk over the roar of the wind outside. The next morning they went outside to discover that theirs was the only shack left standing—twenty other shacks had been swept away during the night. They were surrounded by the Atlantic Ocean.

Another chapter described Chatham's fishermen staying up all night to maneuver their boats back into the ocean after they had been washed into a parking lot covered with ten feet of water and treacherous waves. It described a tuna fishermen catching his breath to dive under the flooded fishing dock to shut off the diesel line before the Chatham Fish Pier building was swept away.

Perhaps I received my greatest compliment when a few years later my son was surfing with Sebastian Junger and Junger swam over to say, "You know, your father's book inspired me to write *The Perfect Storm.*" All things being equal, I wish it had been the other way around!

Hard Times

During the 1980s the federal government created a program to designate twenty-six estuarine research reserves around the coasts of the United States. The program would provide up to $5 million to acquire each reserve and guaranteed them continued funding for long-term research. Pleasant Bay seemed like the ideal location for such a reserve. It was one of the most pristine and undeveloped estuaries on the East Coast. We had already collected ten years worth of baseline data about the bay—research that had also been incorporated into *Shallow Waters* and the *NOVA* film.

But Pleasant Bay had some serious competition. Waquoit Bay, near Woods Hole, was less well known and far less pristine than Pleasant Bay, but it was a lot closer to the scientists who were better at writing proposals than I. I knew that Woods Hole had this edge on the Outer Cape, so I had not paid much attention when they had gone through the preliminary stages of applying for the estuarine designation.

But then I got a wake-up call. As summer approached, the Outer Cape's local paper announced that the last sailing camp was going to close on Pleasant Bay. Traditionally, there had been half a dozen sailing camps on the bay that had kept large tracts of land free from development. Now they were all in the process of closing and developers would soon be in their wake. I was paralyzed with shock. Then it hit me: This could be the perfect event to galvanize the Outer Cape into action. I had already been talking to several environmentalists about creating a local nonprofit organization to support research on Pleasant Bay. Why not create one specifically for applying to become a national estuarine research reserve? I wrote a letter to *The Cape Codder* that said:

There is a strange quiet sadness around Pleasant Bay this morning. No more will we hear the sound of bells marking the beginning of a new day at Viking camp, nor the banter of adolescent kids as they try out brave new snippets of adult language . . . No more will we see the long sleek lines of Viking sail boats as they wend their way down the bay and through the narrows toward the Atlantic Ocean.

Now the land which has lain pristine for all these years will ring with the sounds of chain saws as scores of new homes are built on Pleasant Bay. Does this really have to be? No. If enough people band together we can apply to the federal government to have Pleasant Bay declared a National Estuarine Reserve.

As a piece of writing it was over the top, but it had emerged naturally from my own initial sense of helplessness. Perhaps others had gone through the same emotional seesaw. The letter seemed to strike a deep chord. Everyone could now feel there was at least something we could do to stop this degradation. The movement took on a life of its own. Within two weeks we had over $20,000 in the bank and

300 members in our nascent organization called "The Friends of Pleasant Bay."

But I had moved too quickly. I was an outsider and had not taken the time to get to know the powers that be, nor taken the time to patiently explain that a research reserve would not be a like a big state park. The program has stringent guidelines about the numbers of researchers and students who are allowed to be in a reserve collecting data. But probably it didn't matter. Some wealthy homeowners were soon on their phones, convincing each other that such a reserve would attract untold hordes of daytrippers to invade "our bay and ruin our lifestyle." Before I knew what hit me, they had taken over the nominating committee and voted in the very people who had been the most opposed to both "The Friends of Pleasant Bay" and the reserve. Our small group of environmentalists never had a chance. I learned how difficult it can be to work through a bottoms-up organization where you have to patiently educate people as you proceed. I'm afraid I let the controversy get under my skin and finally resigned, rather than stay to fight the good fight.

The group of retirees who had taken over the organization had their own dilemma: Several hundred people had sent in their hard-earned cash to have the organization do the groundwork to have Pleasant Bay declared a research reserve. Now they expected something. But the directors quietly killed the idea and instead had the state declare the bay an area of critical environmental concern. This was a far cry from a federal program that would have provided millions of dollars to purchase land and conduct long-term research. The public never seemed to notice.

I still smart when I think how much good could have come from the original project. "The Friends of Pleasant Bay" continues to be a powerhouse at raising money. Today it is trying to raise several million dollars to purchase a piece of land crucial to the future health of the bay. It would have been much easier if the group had done this when the federal money was still available. But if it succeeds now, it will have finally lived up to its original potential.

Personally, I learned several lessons from the experience. One was bitter, that craftiness and old age will always win out over youth and competence; one was sweet, that the only thing that has ever changed the world is a small group of determined people. But you have to live through the experience to learn the truth of such clichés.

I had also learned some lessons as a writer. Our words, our research, and our reputations can achieve great things, but we also have to be careful. By nature, we are not very politic. We have a responsibility to stir things up and get things started, but we may not be the right people to do the hard work of getting things done. It is invaluable for a small local environmental organization to have a good writer on board, to raise money and kibitz, but that writer might not be the best person to run the organization!

On a happier note, in 1987 the Marine Biological Laboratory created the MBL Science Writing program to bring science writers to Woods Hole. The program caused an instant sensation. Suddenly this village of people steeped in the rules and strictures of science started to rub shoulders with writers steeped in the rules and traditions of journalism. During the first few years of the program, the MBL presented a series of seminars to explain science to writers and writing to scientists. Most of the seminars had lofty goals and ambitions, but the seminars I liked best were the ones that highlighted the difference between the two cultures.

I remember one writer asking, "What do you do if a scientist you have interviewed asks to see your article before it is published?" That is a common practice in science, where senior scientists are expected to give the final okay to anything going out of their labs. It is understandable that a scientist might think of a writer as just another grad student used to being mistreated. But what would happen if a politician made the same request?

We finally arrived at the following rule of thumb. It's not appropriate for a scientist to ask a writer to review his or her article, but it is okay for a writer to ask a scientist to check an article for factual errors. That may seem like a double standard, but it is actually a pretty good way to bridge the gap between the two cultures.

Conversely, scientists would often complain when writers used the journalist's convention of getting spokespeople to present both sides of a scientific controversy. They argued, quite correctly in my opinion, that the practice gives a faulty picture of the real consensus in a field. But covering science is not like covering politics, where everything is a matter of opinion and there are no independently verifiable data. The problem is becoming more acute in today's world, where economic, political, and religious interests try to pressure journalists into giving equal credence to "both sides" on things like global warming and intelligent design. Presenting both sides often gives readers an inaccurate view of the amount of hard data that supports one side. Presently the religious right has thrown scientists off balance by urging schools to "teach the controversy." As a writer, I've come to the conclusion that it's okay to write about the controversy. The science behind evolution is sound. Why not argue the issue again? The data will speak for themselves. After all, that is the way the scientific method works in scientific journals—why not in the popular press as well?

One of the other issues we addressed was when to use scientific jargon. We decided that even though scientists sometimes use jargon when they don't really understand it, writers have to always understand jargon and never use it!

The seminars were a great success. It was fascinating to see the scientists and writers gradually learning to understand and appreciate the restrictions of each other's worlds. For writers, it was the first time that many of them had the chance to just be with scientists on their home turf. For scientists, it was the first time many realized that the same writer might be called on to write a glowing report of their research one week and do an investigative piece on malfeasance in their labs the next. Science writers are not supposed to be either boosters or detractors of science, just professional journalists covering our beat as best we can.

The program was a revelation for me personally. For years I didn't know whether to call myself an erstwhile scientist or a sometimes writer. Like so many others, I had stumbled into science writing, and now after all that time I finally had a name for who I was and what I did. It was a great relief.

After working so long in isolation, it was good to meet other science writers from publications like the *New York Times* and the *Washington Post*. But I would warn my new-found colleagues that while I loved to share Woods Hole with them in the summer, this village was my territory and they could all just return to their well-paid city jobs in the fall!

Actually, the program reinforced my belief that Woods Hole was the ideal place for a year-round science writing program for recently graduated college students as well as professionals. Here was a small, informal village jam-packed with some of the best scientists in the world. It was commonplace to see Nobel Prize winners casually strolling through town deep in thought or simply intent on catching a striped bass. As a science writer, you had easy access to top scientists in physics, chemistry, oceanography, geology, fisheries, and biomedical research. Local high school students could routinely approach Nobel laureates to discuss their upcoming science projects. Falmouth's annual high school science fair was covered as closely by the local press as the traditional Thanksgiving football game in other areas of the country. It often featured species that were new to science because someone's father had just dredged them up from the deep ocean floor.

My wife was the fortunate recipient of such informality. One day a local reporter happened to overhear Bob Ballard talking about the *Titanic* at his son's high school hockey match. The next day a small article appeared in our paper that had Bob denying that he had any interest in the old wreck.

Kristina was freelancing for national radio at the time and asked Bob if she could come in to do an interview about his research. Bob again denied that he was interested in the *Titanic* but gave her a long interview about the deep-sea technology he had developed for his on-going geological research. After the interview was over, he winked and casually mentioned that Kristina might just want to hang on to the tape. Of course, a few months later, Bob was at sea announcing to the world that he had discovered the *Titanic*. While hundreds of frustrated reporters and television crews crowded around WHOI's lone ship-to-shore receiver, only able to repeat the briefest of announcements, Kristina was able to use her previous interview to produce a detailed program about the technology used to make the discovery. That's the hometown advantage, as comforting to a journalist as the Green Monster is to a Red Sox slugger.

So I had finally realized that Woods Hole would be the ideal place for a year-round science writing program, but I needed to prove the concept would work, so I ran a successful pilot program at the Bermuda

Biological Station. This was in accordance with an age-old Woods Hole tradition that says that marine biologists become particularly interested in problems in tropical oceanography during the months of January, February, and March!

We started the Woods Hole component right after I finished writing *Storm Surge* in 1994. From the beginning we attracted top-notch students who were either going to attend our program or go to graduate school in science, medicine, or journalism. The students said that this was exactly what they were looking for, a program that bridged the gap between science and the humanities and gave them one more year in a liberal arts environment before they had to decide on their future professions.

It was also a slightly subversive program. I hoped that I could convince a few students to become either science writers or at least scientists who could write. Some students relished the idea of being able to write about biology one week and physics the next. Others wanted to be scientists well grounded in their particular fields but also be able to write about it to the widest possible audience.

I was able to place the students in internships working in labs and going out on research cruises. I expected the students to write about their experiences for at least an hour a day, and then we met once a week to discuss their writing. It was a tremendous experience. But it would not last. Kristina had been offered a broadcast job in Boston that was too good to turn down. She made the argument that I could write my books anywhere. I wasn't sure that was true, but had no empirical evidence to the contrary. Besides, our daughter Chappell was about to enter school. I held out for several months in order to finish *Storm Surge* but I finally ran out of excuses. I reluctantly agreed to leave Woods Hole.

Closing our house for the last time was one of the most painful experiences in my life. I made a point of doing most of the final cleanup by myself. It felt like I was in mourning. We had created a unique and purposeful life and had become a part of the community.

I had swept out the house, put the key on the table, and gone outside when I realized I had forgotten one last thing. But it was too late, as the door had clicked shut behind me. It finally hit home: I could never go back into our house again.

Our faithful dog Jake snuggled up unknowingly beside me. *Photo by Kristina Sargent.*

I spent the rest of that warm autumn day sleeping on the beach. Our dog Jake snuggled up unknowingly beside me. He was sick, and we had already decided he would be happier staying on the Cape with some of our friends than moving to the city. He had become such a fixture, sleeping on the warm pavement in front of our house, that neighbors had become accustomed to giving directions by his presence: "Take a left just beyond the black lab sleeping on the road." We didn't think such behavior would translate well to Boston's streets.

The next few years were some of the most difficult of my life. Every time I drove into the city I would feel a heavy depression descend on me as soon as I saw that low gray urban skyline. But I planned to use our time in Boston to write a book about what new developments in brain research could tell us about animal behavior.

When I had studied animal behavior as an undergraduate, we had just considered the brain a big black box. We would come back from the field with observations about how genes affected behavior, but we didn't really know how it was translated by the brain. We knew, for instance, that an animal would act altruistically to protect its kin according to strict Darwinian rules. The animals could calculate with almost mathematical precision just the amount of risk they would be willing to take to save a cousin as opposed to a sister. They did this as accurately as any croupier at a game of roulette, but how did they really do it? We didn't know. But with the advent of new brain imaging technology and knowledge about the role of neurotransmitters, scientists were starting to see how the brain could use intuition and emotion modulated by neurotransmitters to make such accurate, split-second assessments.

I felt that at least our decision to move to Boston would allow me to become really immersed in these new developments. I was hired to teach a science writing course at Harvard and signed up for a neuropsychology course taught by a professor at its medical school. It was a thrill to be back in school, and I loved the challenge of being able to hold my own with all the hotshot undergraduates on their way to medical school.

I also took over much of the job of raising Chappell. I would pick her from school in the afternoon and we would discuss her day over a high tea of milk and cookies. Her days were invariably far more interesting than my own. During the summers we would sneak into the private pool of a neighboring condominium so I could teach her to swim. By the end of the summer the tenants were so sure that we were members that we became quite brazen about evicting other interlopers. There is no bigger thrill than to see your daughter's delight when she takes her first swimming strokes, even if you had to sneak into a private pool to do it.

During this time I was also rocked by personal tragedies. My father died of a heart attack, my mother had a stroke, and my first wife Claudia died from breast cancer. I was depressed and finally entered a program at Massachusetts General Hospital that was conducting clinical trials on timed lights used to treat the effects of seasonal affective disorder. It was fascinating to finally understand how much this condition had shaped my life. I started to understood why my jobs and relationships had always seemed to fall apart in the summers, leaving me bereft and unemployed in the fall. I started to understand that SAD was a double-edged sword. While it made me miserable in the winters, it gave me insight and creative energy in the summers. In fact, I grew to see my writing as a form of self-medication. In the winters it allowed me to forget that I was depressed, and in the summers it kept me more or less out of trouble.

At that time, my writing was in a state of stasis. I simply sat at home writing proposals for books that never went anywhere. After writing a proposal for *The Anxious Brain* and another on my parents' battles with stroke, heart disease, and Alzheimer's, I was desperate. I even decided to give up writing altogether and made an attempt to run for Congress back on Cape Cod. The effort had me driving hundreds of miles a day to regain something I had lost.

I lost the election, but the experience made me realize what an incredible privilege it is to be able to write for a living. In Woods Hole I had started to take it for granted that I would write forever, submitting proposals for books about ever more obscure topics. I was gambling that I could write well enough so that people would be willing to read about whatever subject I chose. It had become something of a sick little hubristic game. Now I couldn't get even the most obvious idea off the ground. I had also succumbed to the idea that I was burned out on writing about the oceans and wanted to cover other topics. I had not counted on the fact that after a while publishers have you pegged as a certain kind of writer and expect more of the same. They knew I could write about nature and marine biology but were not sure I could write about neurobiology.

Gradually things started to fall into place. St. Elizabeth's Hospital asked me to write a book about its surgical training program. I spent so much time watching operations and delving into surgical textbooks that I felt I could perform my own simple little appendectomy. I opened each chapter with a description of an operation and what life was like for the surgeons of each decade of the program that was celebrating its fiftieth year. This was the real story of the hospital that had given its name to television's *St. Elsewhere*. By the end of the book, I felt like I had spent a year in medical school, a path I often thought I might have pursued if I had had the right grades and role models.

It was also during this time that *ER* made its debut on television and producers started to understand the inherent drama involved in medical settings. The National Association of Science Writers and the Sloan Foundation saw the success of the series and sponsored a program to develop a television series that would do for science what *ER* had done for medicine. I won a small prize for submitting an idea about a group of science writers at the *New York Times* who would go out every week to uncover stories about open heart surgery, volcanoes, the raising of a Soviet submarine, or forensic science. Evidently the idea ended up on the bottom of some producer's slush pile, although some of the *CSI* programs share a distant resemblance to some of my story suggestions. It was also interesting to learn that it had taken Michael Crichton twenty years to sell *ER,* and the program reflected what emergency room procedures were like when he wrote the original proposal, rather than what they were like when the program was being produced.

During this time, Kristina and I met Howie Mandell, one of the actors on *St. Elsewhere.* Kristina had grown with up David Morse, who also played a young doctor on the show. Mandell grilled us about Morse's adolescent past. We named names and told of embarrassing incidents. A year later we heard the names of Morse's former girlfriends being announced over the hospital intercom while the actor tried to act like a concerned surgeon hovering over his patient.

I used my final payment for writing the St. Elizabeth's book to buy a ticket to the island of Montserrat. The island's Soufriere volcano had just started to erupt and bury its southern half. My intention was to write an article and prepare a proposal for a book about the fascinating Caribbean island. The proposal was turned down, but it put me in touch with some editors at the Smithsonian Institution who were interested in publishing a book about volcanoes. There is an old saying in science writing circles, that when all else fails, write a book about dinosaurs or volcanoes. I had been writing about unmarketable topics for so long—why not try to write a popular book for a change?

The Smithsonian gave me the credentials to visit volcanoes on Iceland, Sicily, and the Aeolian Islands off Italy. I also put together lectures on the regions, which I showed at schools and colleges. I had started doing this on earlier projects as a way to pay for my research. The lecturing had expanded to the point where I was giving forty or fifty talks a year, and Nikon had donated several lenses and two cameras to me in exchange for the publicity. It was a strange but effective way to support my flagging writing habit. I spent the summer in New Hampshire using all this material to craft a new book proposal. As I wrote the proposal, it gradually dawned on me that volcanoes only present a snapshot in time. They are fascinating, but here I was sitting in New Hampshire surrounded by almost a billion years of history. Her mountains contain three quarters of the history of our planet. It is a complex and subtle story, but if I could tweeze it apart, mountain by mountain, it would make a good book. The story would also force me to get back to basics. I would have to write naturally, write locally, and write about what I knew. It was like returning home after spending so many years wandering about lost, and alone, in the dark.

A Year in the Notch: *Using Science to Write About Nature*
(1998–1999)

In recent years it has become fashionable for writers to say they are sick of nature, or that nature writing, environmentalism, or even nature itself is dead. I disagree, and believe it remains crucial to our species' survival that we continue to write and care about nature.

Part of the problem for this feeling of environmental ennui stems from the fact that so many of today's nature writers majored in English literature rather than science. They go into the field steeped in the writings of Henry David Thoreau and Henry Beston, but would Thoreau and Beston go into the woods today armed only with musty old literary writers as their guides? No, they would have searched the web for the most up-to-date scientific articles and been current on the newest theories in physics, geology, chemistry, and biology.

Thoreau didn't want to be known as the philosopher of Concord, as much as the man whose keen observations of forest succession were better than those of the best botanists of his era. Thoreau, Rachel Carson, and Aldo Leopold were the science writers of their time, science writers who just happened to write about natural history. Their literary fame came later.

I consider it to be a rare privilege to be able to spend several hours a day exploring nature and poring over the scientific literature in an effort to rewrite our ever improving creation myth. When it is going well, writing about nature is a spiritual, almost talmudic experience: You are transported into a joyful, almost meditative state where you are totally in the present: unaware of taxes, bills, and telephone calls. When it is going poorly, the experience is more like opening an artery and watching your blood seep slowly to the floor.

If there is a gene that predisposes humans to believe in a God, there must be an alternative allele for those of us who like to tweak creation myths. The vocation has become more interesting of late, because science, unlike religion, has the unique power to constantly improve our understanding of who we are, and how we got here. The glorious thing for a science writer is that our creation story keeps getting more complex and interesting, and you can retell it whether you are walking through the open fields of nineteenth-century Concord, diving in an estuary on Cape Cod, or scaling the granite cliffs of a mountain in New Hampshire. Every acre of our planet provides a unique new perspective on the intricate dance between life, Earth, and our universe. Writing *A Year in the Notch* allowed me to spend a full year investigating this, the greatest story ever told.

I spent a year driving up to New Hampshire every other week and returning to Boston to write. I would spend a night on Mount Washington, a day in the dank catacombs of the Palermo mine, or an even-ing on Robert Frost's old porch; then I would rush back to the city to scan through the scientific texts and write up and revise my observa-tions. I would have preferred to have spent all my time in New Hamp-shire, but returning to Boston improved my writing. It meant I had to discipline myself to finally stop wandering around doing research and get down to the serious business of writing. I used the formula of "A Year in the Life of the Notch" because it provided me with what aca-demics call a narrative arc. I could write about life and procreation in the spring, abundance and conflicts in the summer, and death and final resolution in the winter. Within that simple story line, I had limitless latitude to discuss almost anything I wanted to write about.

I was able to use a libidinous raccoon to write an X-rated chapter about love and neurobiology among the mammalian line, used the sugaring season and the evening stars to write about new cosmologi-cal theories, and used a simple ceremony to spread my father's ashes during a roguish autumn storm to write about spiritual beliefs.

When you spend every day investigating nature, you cannot help but be awed by the many miracles of the cosmos: the fact that the universe exists, that life got started, that the seasons turn, that all life is related, that you can grow food in the simple soil. But the view you see does not coincide with that of any organized religion. Instead of 10,000 years of orderly creation, you have 14 billion years of big bangs, exploding stars, meteor impacts, ice ages, snowball Earths, extinctions, new spe-cies, and now, a bipedal hominid jury-rigged with a vestigial appendix, bad back, and a single orifice it uses for both procreation and excre-tion. How can all that bumbling be the result of intelligent design?

Yet along with these billions of years of evolution you have an or-ganism, temporarily the apex carnivore on our planet, that seems to be hard-wired into thinking that somebody else, a god, is in charge. But you cannot discount the importance of these spiritual beliefs in guiding human behavior; they are much as you would expect in an intelligent social carnivore. While I remain skeptical that there is a patriarchal god pulling the strings from somewhere up in heaven, I'm more than happy to encourage others to believe what they will, and to pay my own personal obeisance to the wonders of our planet. Others seem to agree. Once I had the unique experience of speaking with the chief of the Wampanoag tribe. I was asking him about Native American beliefs, but he kept putting me off. At one point he pointed to a flower and asked me what it was.

"A lady slipper."

"No, that's a squaw moccasin." To this day I don't know if that was the old Native American term, or if he had been pulling my leg.

But finally when we entered the deep woods he grew serious and said, "Now you can ask your questions. You see, we believe the forest is our church, this is our religion." As one who has always felt my most sacrilegious and uncomfortable in traditional churches, and most moved when surrounded by nature, this struck a deep and abiding chord.

It was also during this time that geologists were starting to publish their findings that more than half a billion years ago our planet plunged into a massive ice age that froze the world's oceans, halted photosynthesis, and nearly extinguished life before it had much of a chance to get started. The only organisms to survive this snowball Earth were simple chemosynthetic bacteria clustered around deep-sea vents where tectonic plates were being formed. Our planet was at a crossroads; it could have tilted either into the icehouse scenario of our neighboring planet Mars, or the hothouse scenario of Venus. It was only through the interaction of geology and life that our planet was saved. Underwater volcanoes belched forth billions of tons of the greenhouse gas into our atmosphere to rewarm our planet, and living organisms thrived to sequester billions of tons of carbon dioxide back onto the ocean floor to cool our planet again. Together, these dual forces of plate tectonics and evolution continue to keep our planet habitable for life. This became the theme and thesis of *A Year in the Notch.*

A chapter on the stars allowed me to mull over Stephen Hawkings provocative statement that "The odds against a universe like ours emerging from something like the Big Bang are enormous." It allowed me to investigate new findings that indicate that everything might not have started with a single Big Bang but that Big Bangs have been occurring for untold billions of years. Most of the Big Bangs probably fizzled out because they had too much antimatter, not enough dimensions, or simply because time in these universes ran backward instead of forward.

Like our planet that just happened to have the right geological and chemical conditions for life, our Big Bang just happened to have the right physical parameters to evolve into stars, planets, and galaxies. Instead of having only a paltry fifteen billion years and a few million planets to work with, evolution had almost an infinite amount of time and untold billions of planets on which it could create life and evolve new species.

Suddenly, with this new theory, our cosmos starts to look a lot older, a little less special, and a lot more probable than before. Instead of having only one chance, we have millions of chances to recycle space, time, energy, and matter into new universes with slightly different properties. The remarkable aspect of this theory is that it suggests that a universe is born, grows, reproduces, and dies. That pretty much fits our definition of life. How many other literary genres allow.you to write about such things in a concrete yet breezy essayist manner?

When I was close to finishing *A Year in the Notch,* I realized I needed one last chapter on ravens. The person to go to for ravens was Bernd Heinrich at the University of Vermont. Dr. Heinrich invited me to spend a weekend in his unheated cabin in Maine. He explained we would have to lug several 200-pound bloody cattle carcasses through the snow to attract and observe his ravens. Unfortunately, our calendars didn't coincide. But when my book came out, Bernd wrote a blurb that said, "A great read! The author takes us on a raucous ride through the New England forest, to see the big picture through unclouded eyes . . . He examines everything in sight and counts it relevant, connecting it with seamless prose into the rational new picture. It's a powerful boost to the new Nature religion that references us to Life on Earth."

I'll take that blurb over a cold weekend in Maine any day. It's an honor to have such an esteemed colleague understand and appreciate what you are trying to do. But if I had succeeded in writing an exuberant, even expansive book, it was only because I was so delighted to get back to using science to write about nature.

Crab Wars: *Investigative Reporting (2000–2001)*

Just as I was finishing *A Year in the Notch,* several Cape Cod papers started running articles about horseshoe crabs. It seemed that the Cape

Cod National Seashore was going to ban harvesting horseshoe crabs in its portion of Pleasant Bay. I hadn't really thought about horseshoe crabs for several years, and here was the issue reappearing at just the right time.

My first reaction had been that closing Pleasant Bay would be the wrong thing to do because it would put pressure on other areas with fewer crabs. The *Cape Cod Times* asked me to write an article on the issue, but as I was doing my research I realized that none of the numbers made any sense. Associates of Cape Cod, the company that was bleeding the crabs, claimed that most of the 60,000 crabs they used every year came from Pleasant Bay. This was impossible. I knew from previous experience that the company would be out of business if it was only bleeding 60,000 crabs a year. In the mid-1980s it was already bleeding 70,000 crabs, and the company had more than doubled in size since then. Where were the missing crabs, and why was the company neglecting to mention them? Then I remembered that in 1985 the company had expanded from catching 35,000 crabs a summer in Pleasant Bay to catching an additional 35,000 from Rhode Island. I started calling Associates of Cape Cod to find out how many crabs the company bled per year, and exactly where its crabs came from. But the company knew I was onto something and issued an edict that its employees were not allowed to take my calls. Of course, this only made me more determined. I continued to call everyone I could think of in the company and felt that most of them were uncomfortable with the policy and wanted to tell their story both honestly and completely.

Finally I got lucky. I was going to be teaching a marine biology course in the summer and wanted to tag some crabs, so I called one of the company's underlings to ask what kind of tag we should use. Evidently he was so low on the totem pole that he hadn't been informed of the edict. As we were talking, he happened to mention that during the peak of their season, Associates of Cape Cod bled up to 1,700 crabs a day. I had to hold my voice steady to finish the conversation. Now it was simply a matter of math. The company had to be collecting at least 70,000 additional crabs in order to have enough to bleed 1,700 crabs a day.

Associates of Cape Cod had failed to mention that almost half of its crabs were now coming from Rhode Island. However, the main thrust of my article was that the federal government should not close Pleasant Bay because it would put pressure on smaller areas less able to support the collecting of crabs for biomedical purposes. I concluded the article by saying that Pleasant Bay's population of horseshoe crabs appeared to be healthy despite twenty-five years of collecting the crabs for the lysate industry, which used their blood to test for Gram-negative bacteria.

Not everyone agreed with my observations. While writing the article I had several conversations with my old friend George Buckley. George was convinced that the population of immature crabs had already crashed in Pleasant Bay. This was based on the number of cast off shells his Harvard students had been collecting for the preceding twenty years. During the late summer the immature crabs would shed their shells and George's students would count them to get an index of how many crabs inhabited the bay. "But George," I argued, "there are plenty of crabs in Pleasant Bay, I've seen them. How can the population of immature crabs possibly be declining? You must have been collecting them at different times during the year, or the wind might have blown them away, or maybe your methodology just stinks!"

Still, something about my article did bother me. The numbers still didn't make sense. If Associates of Cape Cod had been collecting 40,000 crabs a summer, and if they admitted to a 10 percent mortality, they would lose 4,000 crabs the first year, 3,600 crabs the second year, and so on, until after twenty years there should be virtually no crabs left in Pleasant Bay. This would be especially true if George's numbers were correct and the adult crabs were not being replaced by immature crabs. But the bay was undoubtedly full of large female horseshoe crabs. What was going on?

Then I received a call from a friend who had reminded me that a few summers before I had pointed out the unusual number of large crabs and had joked that someone must have been introducing alien crabs into Pleasant Bay as I had done in the eighties. Suddenly it hit me. That was it! Somebody really had been introducing crabs into Pleasant Bay. George and I were both correct. The number of immature crabs had been declining, but nobody had noticed because adult crabs had been introduced, little by little over several years.

Before I dared write anything, I had to convince myself that the crabs really were larger than I remembered them from previous years. This was difficult because neither George nor I had measured the crabs in any systematic way. Then I remembered that Carl Shuster had measured horseshoe crabs up and down the East Coast in the early 1950s. Perhaps he still had his old figures from Pleasant Bay. I called Carl, and he told me the width of the average and largest sized crabs he had measured in Pleasant Bay in 1951.

Armed with these numbers, I drove back down to Pleasant Bay. It was March so the crabs hadn't yet arrived, but their empty shells were still on the beach from the previous summer. I started to measure the shells across the carapace and couldn't believe my eyes. Six out of the twenty crabs I measured were too large to come from Pleasant Bay! I trembled with the same excitement that a scientist must feel when he has just discovered something that no one else has ever known before. But this information presented a problem; it meant that somebody I knew and liked not only had been taking crabs illegally from Pleasant Bay but had been introducing crabs there illegally as well.

Of course, no one was going to believe such a disturbing scenario based on only twenty crabs. A month later, I returned with a dozen high school students and we measured 500 adult crabs, the same number that Carl Shuster had measured in 1951. The results were the same. The male crabs were the same size that they had been in the 1950s because Associates of Cape Cod only bled the large egg-bearing female crabs that held the most blood. But fully a quarter of the female crabs were simply too big to have come from Pleasant Bay. Evidently, tens of thousands of large female crabs had been caught somewhere else, then bled and transplanted to Pleasant Bay to replenish the stock. This was against the Food and Drug Administration regulation that required that all crabs be returned to the waters from which they came. With these numbers in hand, I called the *Boston Globe* science section to see if it wanted an article.

It was not part of my job, but in writing this second article I leaned over backward to be fair to Associates of Cape Cod. I interviewed both Carl Shuster and John Valois from the Marine Biological Laboratory. John said, "I don't think there is a soul who could go down there and point to any evidence that the estuary has been damaged in any major way. Biologically there may have been nothing wrong with transplanting those crabs." Dr. Shuster said, "I think the feds should at least give the company a grace period to line up other sources of crabs."

If that version of my article had run, Associates of Cape Cod would have gotten off almost scot-free. Here were two of the top experts in the field saying they doubted the ecology of the bay had been damaged and that Associates of Cape Cod should be given a chance to find other supplies of crabs.

But then I received a strange telephone call. It was from my editor at the *Boston Globe*. "Bill, we have a problem. I just got a call from the publisher. Apparently his wife met the president of ACC at a cocktail party and now he wants me to kill the story. I told him I believed your version and don't want to kill the story, but said that I would talk to you about having another writer interview ACC to get their side of the story. Would you agree to that?"

I didn't have time to argue. The federal case would be decided any day, and I didn't have time to rewrite the article for another publication, so I agreed. The other writer interviewed Associates of Cape Cod and the story ran without any reference to the introduced crabs.

I had to teach my marine biology course that summer, so I didn't have time to write any more articles. But I felt it was important to get the story out to the public so that other people could see for themselves—everything, the crash in the population of local immature crabs, the importing of adult alien crabs, and the cover-up, including the fudging of numbers as to how many crabs were being bled from where. Time was short, so I committed the journalist's greatest sin. I gave my scoop to another writer!

The *Cape Codder*'s Doreen Leggett had already been approached by Associates of Cape Cod to visit the lab and write a story. But Associates of Cape Cod hadn't expected her to ask any difficult questions. She wrote a special series that ran for two weeks on the front page of the paper. Her articles were far more damaging to Associates of Cape Cod than my original piece would have been.

The series received wide attention and elicited furious letters to the editor. But people were generally more upset about the crabs being introduced than the more important biological problem, that the native population had been decimated by removing the females from the breeding population.

What upset Associates of Cape Cod the most, however, was that the articles revealed that ACC was now owned by a large Japanese pharmaceutical company based in Tokyo. Associates of Cape Cod had conveniently failed to mention this fact in any of its many press releases. I had written about the Japanese ownership, not because Seikagaku was a foreign firm, but because Associates of Cape Cod was no longer the tiny mom-and-pop operation it wanted to appear to be. The facts were all on its web site, available for anyone to see. After the articles appeared, Associates of Cape Cod stopped giving interviews and canceled further press visits to their facility.

I found it interesting that my initial inclination had been to finish the field work I had started working on years before. That was the only way to get the numbers I needed to argue the case in the scientific arena, where the case would be won or lost. The Friends of Pleasant Bay had already weighed in, claiming that my articles were based on anecdotal evidence. But one of their longtime directors made over $100,000 a year collecting the crabs from June through September. He convinced the Friends of Pleasant Bay to raise $65,000 to count the number of horseshoe crabs in Pleasant Bay. This was more money than the federal government or any individual state had ever dedicated toward population studies of horseshoe crabs anywhere up and down the East Coast.

The Friends of Pleasant Bay announced the decision with great fanfare, knowing it would be easy to raise the money for a hotly debated issue about such a charismatic local species. The Cape Cod National Seashore also weighed in, deciding to spend several more thousand dollars to study the horseshoe crabs in Pleasant Bay.

George Buckley and I realized that if there was ever a time to publish our data, this was it. We raised a $200 grant, took two weeks off, and wrote up our twenty-five years worth of research on bleeding mortality, transplanted crabs, and the lack of recruitment caused by removing females during the breeding season. I like to think our $200 paper helped the federal court to decide the case as much as the more expensive studies. Talk about peer review. It is pretty humbling to think your paper must pass the scrutiny of half a dozen high-priced lawyers, let alone a bevy of private and government scientists!

A year after the court upheld the ban, the Friends of Pleasant Bay

Author photo for *Crab Wars*. *Photo by Kristina Sargent.*

released its study, which said that there were half a million adult crabs in Pleasant Bay. If this were true, it would mean Pleasant Bay contained more horseshoe crabs than any other estuary on the East Coast. The researcher had neglected to take into account that horseshoe crabs spend all their summers migrating to and from the spawning beaches. She had spent the entire summer simply recounting the same crabs as they crossed and recrossed her grid!

Once our paper was finished, I realized that my role should be as a writer, even though doing field work had been a lot more fun. But the controversy had become so convoluted that simple articles were no longer sufficient. Finally it dawned on me that the history of the lysate industry would make for a small but important book, because the story of horseshoe crabs would provide me with a vehicle to write a morality play about the unintended consequences of biotechnology.

I also realized I that was uniquely qualified to write the book. I had grown up on Pleasant Bay, where I had found the ungainly creatures intrinsically fascinating. I knew that the discovery of *Limulus* lysate was the most important discovery to come out of marine biology, but I also knew that some of the lysate companies had cut corners to get to the top. I had interviewed students at Harvard Business School's

class on entrepreneurship to learn the financial aspects of the industry. Their numbers had helped me when I wanted to calculate how
many crabs the companies had to bled in order to sell $10 million of
lysate a year at $50 a pop. I had even gotten myself into a fair amount
of hot water in the eighties working for Associates of Cape Cod in
order to figure out the inside story.

Writing *Crab Wars* allowed me to interview extraordinary people
and visit fascinating locations up and down the East Coast. Carl Shuster had spent his entire career dissecting the behavior of horseshoe
crabs from Cape Cod to Florida. Fredrik Bang had stumbled upon the
lysate reaction serendipitously when a crab had accidentally sludged
up and died in his Woods Hole lab. Stan Watson had colorfully broken away from the strictures of science to plunge into the heady world
of biotechnology, and Brian Harrington had banded migratory birds
from the barrens of Tierra del Fuego to the frozen tundra of the Arctic Circle.

Each location had its own story to tell, the Nobel Prize-winning
research of the quiet village of Woods Hole, the hurricanes and ponies
of Chincoteague Island, and the migratory shorebirds who consumed
248 tons of horseshoe crab eggs during their two-week stopover on
the beaches of Delaware Bay. The book allowed me to explore the bu-
reaucratic wrangling and the wheeling and dealings of the Centers for
Disease Control, the Food and Drug Administration, and the Joseph
Moakley Federal courthouse in Boston. I even explained the role horseshoe crabs had played in what has been described as modern medicine's most flagrant miscalculation, the political decision to inoculate
every man, woman, and child against the swine flu epidemic. The epidemic never occurred, and hundreds of people were killed or left neu-
rologically damaged by the contaminated vaccine. President Ford had
followed the advice of his Secretary of Defense, Donald Rumsfeld, then
known for being the youngest man to hold that office, now known for
being the oldest man to ever hold that office.

I had to recreate many barely remembered conversations to relate
this story. At the time, no one had thought their long-ago conversations would be memorable, and nobody had bothered to take notes.
I tried to remedy the situation by interviewing as many people as I
could reach to compare their memories of each conversation. But many

of the participants had already died, so I had to rely on the recollections of their widows, wives, and colleagues. I also spent long hours poring through the morgues of local newspapers and driving to Boston to transcribe the transcripts of the federal court case between the Department of Interior and Associates of Cape Cod and another case between Associates of Cape Cod and its former chief scientist.

The Internet has made this kind of sleuthing much easier. Instead of driving all the way to Virginia to get details of a hurricane that had almost destroyed an early lysate company on Wallops Island, I could just go online and download precise details about exactly how high the water had risen in the Methodist church in Chincoteague and how many people had poled their boats down Main Street. These are the kinds of details that make a story come alive.

I also found that my writing and speaking became more hardheaded. Instead of using moral and aesthetic persuasion, I started making economic and species-centric arguments. Now I open my talks by asking, "Is there anyone in the room who thinks their life has been saved by a horseshoe crab?" Pause.

"No? Well, is there anyone in the room who would have had a flu shot in 2004 but didn't because it was found to be contaminated?" Half of the hands go up.

"Now, how many of you have ever had a flu shot, surgery, of received intravenous fluid? Okay, the lives of everyone who raised their hands because they would have had a flu shot were *saved* by horseshoe crabs. The lives of everyone has ever had a flu shot, surgery, or intravenous fluid have been *protected* by horseshoe crabs. Anything that is going to come in contact with the human blood system has to be tested against Gram-negative bacteria, and the way that is done is with horseshoe crab blood."

This simple exercise brings home the point that the horseshoe crab test is one of the most commonly used medical procedures in use today and it is entirely dependent on a single species of wild animal—a species that is declining up and down the East Coast.

Next I make the economic argument that if you keep a horseshoe crab alive, it is worth $2,500 over its lifetime for lysate, but if you chop it up and use it dead for bait it is only worth about 70 cents a pound. These arguments make more sense to more people than the fact that shorebirds are dependent on horseshoe crab eggs or that the crabs are just so inherently cool.

Just as I was finishing my book, everything changed. I was interviewing the former chief scientist of Associates of Cape Cod when he mentioned that a plane had just torn into the side of the World Trade Center. Like the rest of the world, I hung up stunned, and sat at home for the rest of the day numbly watching video of the planes ripping into the Twin Towers, the Pentagon, and an abandoned field in Pennsylvania. I picked up my daughter at school, called my son in Brooklyn, and wondered, what was I doing writing a book about horseshoe crabs when the world was falling apart? It became worse a few weeks later when somebody started sending anthrax through the mail.

Then it hit me: I was doing something important. Every batch of vaccine used against bioterrorism was going to have to be tested with *Limulus* lysate. I changed my title from *Bleeding the Crab* to *Crab Wars: A Tale of Horseshoe Crabs, Human Health, and Bioterrorism.* In my preface I quoted John Steinbeck, who had experienced the same doubts during World War II when he had been writing a book about collecting marine animals with his mentor, the biologist Ed Ricketts. Steinbeck wrote about their taking a tiny colony of corals from a tidal pool and how it was important to the corals but not very important to the pool itself. He wrote that Japanese fishing boats then dredging up tons of shrimp were important to the shrimp but not very important to the Pacific Ocean. He wrote that the bombs that were then falling throughout the world was important to our planet, but that "the stars were not moved thereby." He wrote that it was all important or none of it was very important at all. I thought about Steinbeck's words as the days unfolded. Gradually it dawned on me that I had been doing something important. I had been writing about an animal that has been on our planet three hundred times longer than our own species. I was honoring an animal that has saved almost a million more human lives than had died in the World Trade Center. I was writing about caring for our precious planet that we think we can bomb with impunity to achieve safety from members of our own species—people genetically identical to ourselves.

I was trying to show the miracle of the universe, the miracle that all life is related, the miracle that all people are part of the same contentious family, the reality that we must find a way to live together on our teeming wonderful planet or destroy it for all eternity. In my own way, I was praying that that would never happen.

Vaccine Chronicles: *The Book That Never Got Published* (2001–2002)

Every author has a book that never got published. Mine was written right after 9/11. New York was still smoldering, and anthrax was making its presence felt in our local post office. Like most Americans, I was initially so shocked by the cascade of events that all I could do was stay home and watch television. But slowly I started to look around to see what I could do to help. I was too old to go to Afghanistan, and my writer's physique would only get in the way at Ground Zero. But I did know how to write.

The anthrax mailings of September 18 and October 9, 2001, displayed how vulnerable we had been to an attack from this long lasting biological weapon. How much more vulnerable would we be to fast spreading virus like smallpox? Soon after the mailings, President Bush announced that the federal government would provide funding for the production of enough vaccines and antibiotics to thwart such attacks.

If both the federal government and private industry were going to swing into action, it was clear that there was going to be intense competition between scientists for grants, and companies for contracts. A Canadian manufacturer was already offering to give the United States free supplies of generic antibiotics in order to undercut Bayer Aspirin's monopoly on Cipro, the drug of choice against anthrax. It was clear that this was going to be a major business and scientific story.

I had just written about the competition between the companies making horseshoe crab lysate; why shouldn't I take on this far more topical story? If nothing else, I would be writing about something everyone was actually reading about. Perhaps I could even dine out on my expertise. I rushed to put together a proposal for *The Vaccine Chronicles,* a book that would investigate the push to develop vaccines against bioterrorism. Word spread quickly as the proposal circulated through various publishing houses. But I didn't have time to negotiate.

I wanted to concentrate on writing the entire book except for the last two chapters, then wait to see what we would find in Iraq.

So instead of spending too much time haggling with publishers who were unfamiliar with my work, I submitted my proposal to a former editor who had just been hired to revitalize the University of Michigan's academic press. It wouldn't be able afford a large advance but I felt that didn't matter; the book would be so timely that I would be able to recoup my expenses from future sales. Besides, it felt a little unseemly to be quibbling about advances during a time of national crisis.

The book showed that the United States has always had ambivalent feelings about biological weapons. During the early sixties, biological weapons were considered to be more humane than conventional weapons. The Pentagon had even concocted a secret project, code-named the Marshall Plan, to spray a cocktail of three powerful viruses over the island of Cuba. The combined force of the agents would leave the island's inhabitants so convulsed with a succession of fevers, headaches, and crippling diarrhea that U.S. soldiers could move in quickly and pacify the island with no loss of life. President Nixon, under pressure from opposition to the war in Vietnam, made the political decision to renounce the use of biological weapons and sign the International Convention Against Biological and Chemical Weapons.

In many ways, this grand gesture was the start of the modern world's problems with biological warfare. The Soviet Union never believed that the United States had actually stopped making biological weapons, so it continued to make its own. Plus, a small group of American policymakers and scientists thought the United States should never have given up such useful weapons. They became know in Washington circles as the "bugs and gas boys." By the 1990s the "bugs and gas boys" held influential positions in the State Department, the CIA, and the administrations of Presidents Clinton and, later, President Bush and Vice President Cheney. And the bugs and gas boys were still working to get the United States back into the business of making biological weapons.

My source for the chapters on the Soviet Union's biological warfare program was none other than the former head of the Soviet Union's biological warfare unit called Biopreparat. Ken Alibek had defected to the United States after the collapse of the Soviet Union. I never believed I would be able to get through to Dr. Alibek, but one day I just called him at his office in Virginia, and who should answer but Dr. Alibek himself. He was just as open and charming over the phone as in his book *Biohazard*. Soon I was talking to Ken almost as much as I was talking to my family. I never thought I would be on a first name basis with someone who used to be driven through the darkened streets of Moscow with two KGB agents in tow.

By the 1970s, the Soviet Union had stockpiled over 20 tons of smallpox, enough to fill several fleets of ICBM missiles targeted at the West. At the same time, the Soviet Union's doctors had been busy perfecting Soviet medicine, with its emphasis on vaccination. After eradicating smallpox in the Soviet Union, they convinced the World Health Organization to initiate a highly successful international program to rid the world of this ancient scourge.

But what happened to the Soviet Union's biological weapons after the breakup of the Soviet Union? This is where the story became really interesting. Like a few other scientists, Ken Alibek defected to the United States, where he started a multimillion-dollar vaccine research company, thus cementing his success under both the communist and capitalist systems.

Other scientists appeared to be willing to sell their expertise to different countries, including South Africa, North Korea, Cuba, Jordan, Syria, and Iraq. It was President Clinton who realized that these biological weapons could be great equalizers, providing rogue states and independent operators like Osama bin Ladin with weapons that were just as deadly and a lot less expensive than the nuclear weapons controlled by the more powerful First World nations.

There were classified documents and articles in reputable journals that indicated that former Soviet scientists had sold their wares. I wrote a chapter based on a story in the *New York Times* that a female virologist from Zagorsk had been seen in Baghdad, presumably selling biological weapons. Another chapter was based on a story that appeared in the *Atlantic Monthly* about Muhammed Jaward who supposedly smuggled biological weapons hidden in refrigerator motors from Iraq to Al-Quaeda operatives in Afghanistan in 2000. Another document showed that after the first Gulf War, Saddam Hussein had been willing to forego billions of dollars in the United Nations Oil for Food program in order to keep his weapons of mass destruction. They would enable him to destroy Israel, thus securing his place as the modern unifier of the Muslim world. The CIA used these stories to bolster their psychological profile of Saddam Hussein, which indicated that he would never give up what he called his "holy weapons." It was probably their belief in this psychological profile that allowed people in the Administration to convince themselves that Hussein still had weapons of mass destruction, though there was scant evidence to support the conclusion.

Of course, we are now learning that the source of most of the evidence for Iraq's biological weapons came from an elusive informant called "Curveball" and the equally unreliable Ahmed Chalabi. The stories had been leaked to reporters like Judith Miller of the *New York Times,* who is presently involved with the CIA leak investigation for refusing to identify her sources for other articles.

But something else didn't make sense. Who was the anthrax mailer? Almost every scientist I interviewed was convinced that it was a scientist at the U.S. Army's Fort Detrick Biological Warfare Defense Institute in Maryland. Stephen Hatfill had been implicated in an anthrax attack in Zimbabwe and had been rumored to have instigated two hoax anthrax attacks to secure himself a job at Fort Detrick. There was also a story in the *New York Times* that reported that Hatfill had been pulled over by the FBI while driving a model biological weapons lab from the Dugway testing grounds in Utah to Camp LeJeune, where it would be used to train commandos to dismantle the mobile labs we expected to find in Iraq. Supposedly Hatfill, already under suspicion for the mailings, flashed the FBI agents a CIA badge and was waved on. Was he just being a good soldier? A leading member of the American Federation of Scientists thinks that the FBI wanted to keep Hatfill dangling so they could smoke out the person higher up in the hierarchy who had looked the other way, as Admiral Poindexter had done when Oliver North transferred money from the Iranians to the Contras in Honduras.

Suddenly I felt like I was back at the Law of the Sea conference. Were we being bamboozled again? Five people had died and twenty more had come down with anthrax. The mailer had written a note warning his victims that they had been exposed to anthrax and to take antibiotics right away. If the anthrax mailer was working for a higher purpose, it was not an unprecedented situation. During World War II, several civilians had died when the Pentagon had sprayed plant bacteria over San Francisco in a simulated but secret biological attack.

Under the stewardship of John Bolton, the United States withdrew from the Biological Weapons Treaty and Congress voted $5.6 billion to combat bioterrorism. The way we are going to do that is to build six level-four biocontainment facilities in major metropolitan areas like Boston, hurricane-prone Galveston, and San Francisco. Thousands of graduate students will be trained in these facilities to culture diseases for which there are no vaccines and no known cures. Formerly this kind of research was only done by military personnel in secure central locations like Fort Detrick. Now it is going to be done by hundreds of graduate students scattered around the country. Does that make you feel any more secure?

Is something fishy going on here? One thing *The Vaccine Chronicles* had taught me was that you can't have a biological weapon until you have a vaccine against it. If not, the agent can blow back onto your own troops, as tularemia had done against the Soviets in the Battle of Stalingrad. Had the "bugs and gas boys" finally gotten their way? Will the United States use Bioshield's biocontainment facilities as a way of getting back into the business of making biological weapons through the back door?

I simply couldn't say. I didn't have a "Deep Throat." I didn't have an advance large enough to camp out in Washington and use the Freedom of Information Act to pry out the answers. I was using secondhand stories from sources like the *New York Times* and the *Atlantic Monthly,* and it was turning out that most of the stories had been fed to the writers by shady guys like "Curveball" and Ahmed Chalabi. Was I onto something, or not? I simply didn't know. Unlike in *Crab Wars,* I was too removed from the action to know who was lying and who was telling the truth.

For better or worse, the dilemma was finally taken out of my hands. The University of Michigan Press had sent my manuscript around to several experts. They were dismayed that I had written several chapters in the present tense as if had been writing a screenplay. They felt my book would be more academic if I had written it all in the past tense. Some felt my writing had been conspiratorial, others that I didn't know where I was going. But most of all, no biological weapons of mass destruction had shown up in Iraq. The issue was going to be off everyone's radar screen. The book was canceled.

It had taken me over a year of painstaking research to write *The Vaccine Chronicles*. Should I have tried to dispute the ruling? I think not. When something like this happens, the best thing to do is just get back on your horse and start writing another book. Frankly, I had also become sick of writing about the dreary topic. Besides, we had just moved to Ipswich, Massachusetts, and I was eager to get back to writing naturally.

The House on Ipswich Marsh *(2003–2004)*

A few weeks after 9/11, my wife was at our apartment in Charlestown, my daughter was swimming at the Boys and Girls Club, and I was walking our dog around the Bunker Hill Monument. It was a warm sultry autumn evening. The lights of Boston spread out below us and the Zakim Bridge rose majestically over the problems of the Big Dig. I listened to the concerns of the twenty-something-year-olds as a motley assortment of yuppie and townie dogs marked their respective territories.

Suddenly half the lights of Boston went out and police cars started to converge on Charlestown from every section of the city. Everyone thought the same thing. The liquified natural gas facility in nearby Chelsea was a known terrorist target. Every week liquefied natural gas (LNG) tankers from the Middle East steamed into Boston Harbor and all other boat traffic had to come to a complete halt. Military craft bristling with submachine guns escorted the tankers into port as helicopters hovered overhead and the state police stopped all automobile traffic from crossing the Tobin Bridge. Everyone knew that if one of the LNG tankers were ever hit, a massive fireball could envelop the entire metropolitan area.

I ran to the Boys and Girls Club, where groups of children were excitedly milling about the streets, waiting for their worried parents.

I scooped up my daughter and raced back to our darkened apartment. Sitting around flickering candles, my daughter, my wife, and I admitted to each other that none of us had been very happy since leaving Woods Hole. It was decided, then and there, that we would move back to the country. But where?

When I was in college, my best friend used to invite me to his parents' home in Ipswich, Massachusetts. It was a secret jewel. Ipswich had the same extensive marshes and broad beaches as found on Cape Cod, but they were only forty miles north of Boston. Several years later, when I was negotiating with *NOVA* to make a film about an estuary, the producers were considering two locations, the Great Marsh in Ipswich or Pleasant Bay on Cape Cod. Since I had set up a lab on Pleasant Bay and already had spent ten years of my life studying her waters, I lobbied pretty hard for the Cape Cod location. After winning the argument, however, I filed the idea into the back of my mind that someday Ipswich would be a pretty good place to explore. Perhaps that day had arrived.

We started renting a small cottage on a drumlin overlooking Ipswich Bay. Every weekend I would kayak down the bay's steep-sided tidal creeks and explore her hidden islands. Her marshes were alive with the soft calls of willet and the quiet murmuring of her fertile tidal flats. There was definitely a book to be written about this rich and productive area.

But things don't always turn out as planned. I thought I would write a book about the marine biology of the marsh, but each time we drove out to the cottage we passed a beautiful open field. It was a long, broad field surrounded by lush green marshes. A red open-doored barn sat on a distant hill dotted with pear and apple trees. Orioles flitted from blossom to blossom.

I'm afraid I trespassed rather egregiously to explore the old farm and even made some not-so-subtle inquiries as to the availability of the property. It turned out that the house was indeed for sale, but at a price that was far beyond what we could afford. But a year later my wife was looking through the *Boston Globe* and spotted a photograph of a large old pink house nestled beside a swale of phragmites. A buxom mermaid acted as a door knocker and each bathroom looked like a set for *The Little Mermaid*. It was about as environmentally and aesthetically incorrect an image as could possibly be conceived: a 1740 colonial house painted pink, surrounded by the one of the most invasive species known to mankind. But there it was, large, pink, and utterly charming.

As our real estate agent drove us up to visit the house, I realized that it sat on a corner of the same field I had fallen in love with the year before. I was supposed to have fallen in love with a marsh, but I had fallen in love with this field instead, and as every writer knows, there is just no accounting for love—nor how it will change your life. We weren't in the market to buy a house, but there it was: wisteria, hollyhocks, a white picket fence bedecked with hundreds of pink and white roses—how could we possibly refuse?

The day we moved in, the Ipswich Conservation Commission announced that it was going to build a six-car parking lot right beside our back door. I swung into action, writing letters, protesting, making a general nuisance of myself. In the process, I learned a lot more about the ecology of the field and even received a small grant to study the bobolinks who nested there.

Over time, my natural interests changed from the ecology of the marsh to the biology of the pasture. My tussles with the conservation commission improved my focus. The political process finally ended when I had to speak in front of the entire board of selectmen against the conservation commission. It was a strange situation for an environmentalist to find himself in.

The setup reminded me of a time in the sixties when I was driving the Harvard debating team through the Deep South. As we entered Lake Charles, Louisiana, we passed under a huge banner announcing the annual Lake Charles Community College versus Harvard University foreign policy debate. At that night's lavish banquet we were given our topic, resolved "that the United States should abandon Vietnam," and met the panel of judges who would judge our performance—the chief of police, the head of the fire department, the owner of the local gun store, and the chairman of the Lake Charles board of selectmen. We lost the debate, four to zero, as Harvard had traditionally done for the past twenty-five years. I figured my chances were just about as good as the new kid on the block in Ipswich. They were, and I lost, but I had gained a storyline for my upcoming book.

Ready to kayak. Author photo for *The House on Ipswich Marsh*. *Photo by Kristina Sargent.*

All this was going on as I was trying to finish *The Vaccine Chronicles*. I would never advise a writer to move, buy a house, or get involved in a local political dispute while trying to write a book. If you do, remember you still have to keep churning out your requisite five to ten pages a day. It does remarkable things for clearing the brain of extraneous concerns.

I finally did finish my manuscript for *The Vaccine Chronicles*, submitted it, and waited for a response. After a few days of hearing nothing, I decided to use my time to write up a proposal for *The House on Ipswich Marsh*. I soon found myself in the enviable position of having two publishers bidding against each other for the proposed book. Frankly, when *The Vaccine Chronicles* was eventually turned down it was not a total disappointment. I was eager to put the depressing subject behind me and plunge into this new and exciting project. It is also a tightly guarded writers' secret that it is a lot more fun to start a new book than to finish a tired old one.

I was also able to negotiate a clause in my contract that stipulated that I would be reimbursed for doing my own publicity. When you are trying to make a living off of writing local books, this is critical. There is a niche for such books, and you can make a living at it, but you have to be willing to shoulder a lot of the publicity work. If your out-of-pocket expenses are being paid, so much the better.

Some well-known authors complain about having to go on book tours, but I think this is really just a subtle form of boasting. Personally, I find it refreshing to talk to a real live human being after spending all day talking to an empty piece of paper. Of course, I am lucky—I don't have to fly halfway across the country and stay in a series of lonely little motels. I can usually write in the mornings and sign books in a neighboring village in the afternoons. I also find it reassuring that if I need some extra money, I can always pile a few extra boxes of books into my car and drive down to Cape Cod or up to Maine to sell them.

I have also learned that I can give a decent illustrated lecture but am lousy at readings. Since I take photographs to accompany most of my books anyway, it is easy to develop a lecture for each book. I also find that lecturing helps my writing by forcing me to come up with clear and succinct ways to explain difficult topics to a sometimes restive audience. This is important because science writers have to develop short but accurate ways of explaining difficult concepts without interrupting the flow of their narrative. It is a kind of shorthand that, if well-developed, allows you to avoid jargon and be both accurate and stylish at the same time.

It turned out that *The House on Ipswich Marsh* was exactly what the public wanted to read after 9/11 and what I wanted to write. It became a nostalgic book about our pastoral past and an optimistic book about our shared future.

In most of my books I like to include a charismatic species as a main character that I can return to throughout the narrative. These main characters have included horseshoe crabs, sow bugs, bobolinks and ticks; some may argue with my choice of charismatic species, but there it is. In this book our house became the main character. It harkened back to an era when New England was dotted with such houses in such small simple agrarian communities. But the house also provided me with a vehicle to investigate the deeper past. I had to keep reminding myself that the occupants of our house had been citizens of the British Empire for almost as long as they had been citizens of the United States, and that the beams supporting our house had been saplings only a few years after Columbus had discovered America.

The first owner of our house churned butter in our basement dairy, while commiserating with her neighbor, who had lost twelve children to smallpox in a single year. Her husband hauled tons of boulders from our field to build causeways across the marsh so his oxen wouldn't sink into the soft peat while pulling hay. I often think of Captain Smith in ninety-degree weather, working behind his sweating oxen while greenheads, deer flies, midges, and mosquitoes swarmed around their heads.

Someone buried a cache of Revolutionary era rifles under our backyard garden, and a former owner found arrowheads and fishing sinkers beside a spring that still bubbles out of the ground near the back corner of our lot. Paleo-Indians once slaughtered woolly mammoths at nearby Bull Brook when this coast was rising out of the ocean at the rate of nine inches a year as the glaciers were retreating. This meant that this coast was gaining thirty-six feet of new land every year, almost as much as New Orleans loses in an average year and the amount we lost during the 2005 northeaster that decimated our dunes and caused the most widespread outbreak of red tide to ever hit New England.

Finally, this caprice of geology on which our house now sits started out as an arc of volcanic islands that erupted off the supercontinent of Rodinia when it was situated over what we now call the South Pole. It has taken almost a billion years for the forces of plate tectonics to push and pull this suspect terrane, at the speed your fingernail grows, 30,000 miles to its present location on the North Shore of Massachusetts!

The House on Ipswich Marsh also looked ahead. I described Ipswich children using the scientific method to census alewives and study vernal pools. I discussed the arrival of New England Biolabs, a new biotechnology firm that will hire some of these same kids to develop pharmaceuticals to help save lives and keep our town vibrant.

One day when I was working on *The House on Ipswich Marsh*, I discovered some red barberry bushes at the edge of our field. Few people recognize them now, and modern field guides only give them short shrift, but I happened to stumble on a reference to barberries in one of the later writings of Henry David Thoreau. Thoreau described throngs of people clambering over the hills of Concord to pick barberries for jams, jellies, and medicine. I have to admit that at first I thought he was using an old spelling for blueberries. Then I discovered that barberries had been transplanted from Europe until observant colonists discovered that barberry bushes always seemed to be associated with outbreaks of wheat rust. Whenever you had a wheat field surrounded with barberries, the wheat developed the ugly fungus. Some historians have even speculated that the girls who fingered the Salem witches were themselves victims of hallucinations brought on by the ergot-like infected grain.

Today we would describe barberries as being vectors or carriers of the wheat rust fungus. But the most fascinating aspect of this story is that farmers recognized that barberries were carriers of wheat rust years before the scientific world had discovered that germs cause diseases and can be passed on from one species to another. However, this was such common knowledge in the 1700s that several colonies passed laws that made farmers remove any barberry bushes that grew around their wheat fields.

I found myself going back to Thoreau for other reasons as well. Frankly, when I was forced to read Thoreau as a student I had not been very impressed. Who cared how much he paid for nails to build his house on Walden Pond, and why did we have to read about civil disobedience when we were doing it every day anyway?

But in doing research for *The House on Ipswich Marsh* I read some of the later works of Thoreau written at the end of his career, when he wanted to make a significant contribution to science. From his observations of the fields, farms, and woodlots around Concord, he deduced that plant succession was not a straightforward progression from an open field to a specific climax forest mostly dominated by a single species of trees. This was the reigning scientific opinion of his day, but Thoreau recognized that the New England environment was a richly dynamic place and that what kind of landscape came first would determine what kind of landscape would follow. Former wheat fields might lead to hardwoods, open pastures to pines, and woodlots to a variegated mixture of the two.

I knew this story intimately because I seem to have had a relative on the wrong side of almost every artistic and scientific debate. Theodore Roosevelt hired my great-uncle to survey the forests of North America and make recommendations for their recovery. George Sprague

Sargent determined that most of North America had once been covered with large tracts of towering pine forests and that pines were the desired climax species. Had he read the later writings of Thoreau, the former head of the Arnold Arboretum would have know that pine trees do not beget pine trees, because young pine trees cannot grow in the shade of old pine trees. The saplings that thrive below pine trees are hardwoods. In other words, you have to have an open pasture before you can start growing viable pine trees.

The result of all this misinterpretation was that government workers spent years trying to plant pine trees where hardwoods wanted to grow. Predictably, their efforts failed until they finally realized that large tracts of pine trees are accidents of history—the result of land clearing by the glaciers, Native Americans, or farmers that came before.

Had Uncle George paid more attention to his Thoreau, he might have avoided the embarrassing debacle. But it was not entirely his fault. Thoreau's scientific writings were largely ignored because he had been labeled the "philosopher of Concord," and who was going to take the word of a philosopher when designing a forestry plan?

My uncle's mistake made me realize that my own career has rather inadvertently copied Thoreau's. We have both written almost exclusively about New England. In my own case, "the apple had not fallen very far from the tree" out of economic necessity. I'm not so sure about Henry David's.

To my mind, Thoreau's best works were not his preachy opinions, but his detailed observations about the interactions between the people, agriculture, and New England's remaining wilderness areas. Thoreau bemoaned the fact that New Englanders were clearing the land and destroying wilderness. Now here I was, bemoaning the fact that New Englanders had destroyed the nineteenth-century pastoral New England that Thoreau had witnessed, but celebrating the fact that wilderness, in the guise of turkey, deer, moose, bear, coyotes, and reforestation, was returning.

In the same way that Thoreau realized he was writing about a rapidly changing environment, I hope I have provided an accurate snapshot of New England as it is being changed by global warming, urban sprawl, reforestation, and suburbanization. I have written about rural areas, primarily because I love them, but also because that is where most of the decisions we will have to make to save our environment will be made and where they will have their greatest impact. Every town should have their own cranky local Thoreau to urge this process along.

I like to think that some of my books have made a small difference in saving our environment: perhaps a new park here, a more rational policy there. But I also hope my writing shares something else with Thoreau's. I have tried to write books that are accurate snapshots of life on a rapidly changing planet. If someone were to pick up one of my books fifty or a hundred years hence and say, "Oh, so that's what New England was really like, back in the good old twenty-first century," then I will know I have finally succeeded.